GOING TO GOD FOR HELP WITH YOUR
HABITS, **GOALS**, AND **EMOTIONS**

THE
RENEWING
OF THE
MIND
PROJECT

BARB RAVELING

TRUTHWAY PRESS

Truthway Press
Copyright © 2015, 2016 Barb Raveling
All rights reserved.

First printing February 2015
Second printing December 2016

This book is not intended as a substitute for the advice of professional counselors. If you are struggling with a serious issue, please do so under the guidance of a professional counselor and/or physician.

Cover design and layout by Steven Plummer, SPBookDesign.com

Dewey decimal number: 248.4

ISBN: 0-9802243-5-7
ISBN-978-0-9802243-5-1

Table of Contents

QUESTIONS AND BIBLE VERSES

Starting a Habit or Pursuing a Goal

This is so boring. I don't want to do it.

I don't know what to do so I'll do nothing.

This isn't going as well as I thought. Is it worth it?

I really don't want to do this.

I shouldn't have to do this. I've already done enough.

Letting Go of Negative Emotions

Stopping a Habit

I need a little excitement in my life.

It's not a big deal if I break my boundaries.

Everything's going wrong. I really, really need this.

I need this.

I deserve this.

CHAPTER 1

The Secret of Transformation

I STILL REMEMBER THE moment I became a Christian. I was in a huge auditorium, as high up in the stands as you could get, and David Wilkerson was asking me to come to the front of the arena.

People were streaming to the stage, and God was whispering, "Are you willing to be embarrassed for me?" I debated . . . and then I said yes. I left my friend and trudged down the never-ending flight of stairs. I wanted Jesus, and I was willing to do anything to get Him. And at that moment, anything meant walking down those stairs.

As the auditorium filled with thousands of voices singing "I Have Decided to Follow Jesus," I surrendered my life to God. And in the midst of a crowd of hugging and crying people, it felt like He was wrapping me in a blanket of love.

I was so excited to be a Christian. So excited to know Jesus. So excited to begin our relationship.

The next day I jumped on my bike and pedaled downtown to the Christian bookstore. After buying a yellow and orange Living Bible and a booklet by Leighton Ford called "Letters to a New Christian," I hurried home to begin reading.

Jesus did not disappoint. He was everything I thought He would be and more. I loved spending time with Him. Loved reading my Bible. Loved just sitting with Him.

As vividly as I remember those early days, I have no recollection of when I started to walk away from God. I don't remember when quiet times became a drudgery rather than a delight. Or when the same goal began surfacing year after year on my New Year's resolutions list: start having quiet times.

Like the church in Ephesus, I had lost my first love. And even though that love came back sporadically over the next twenty-five years, for the most part it was a duty-driven relationship.

Don't get me wrong—I was still a "good Christian." I went to church, stayed away from the Christian no-nos, and even led Bible studies. But I wasn't in love with God, and I wasn't experiencing victory over my habits and sins.

I was beginning to feel like I would *never* change when God stepped in. He showed me the secret, not only to breaking free from my bad habits and sins, but also to a closer walk with Him. The secret is found in Romans 12:2: *Do not be conformed to the world, but be transformed by the renewing of your mind.*

How did I miss that verse? It told me what to do if I wanted to change. The only thing I can say in my defense is that I was blinded by unrealistic expectations. You see I was expecting God to change me automatically—with no effort on my part.

So when I read Romans 12:2, I wasn't thinking, *Oh, I need to spend some time actively renewing my mind if I want to be transformed.* I was thinking, *Oh, isn't that great? God is going to change me and cure me of all my bad habits.*

After all, I was a Christian. Isn't that what God did for Christians?

I waited . . . and waited . . . and waited . . . but nothing happened. Each year ended the same way it began. Same old bad habits. Same old unmet goals. Same old me.

So I took matters into my own hands. Surely I could drum up enough willpower for a few minor changes: Learn to be nice, for example. Stop complaining. Have a regular quiet time.

As it turns out, no, I couldn't. My new strategy was just as ineffective as my old strategy. Instead of relying on God's strength, I was relying on my own—and I was a weakling in the strength department.

Renew Your Mind

Nothing worked until I started doing what the Bible was telling me to do all along: I started to renew my mind. Consistently, diligently, and expectantly. And that's when God began to change me.

Not overnight, but slowly and steadily, so that now, looking back on fourteen years of consistently renewing my mind, I can see changes in my thoughts, emotions, and behavior that I never would have thought possible in the old days of constant defeat.

I was so grateful to God for what He had done in my life that I began to write. And now three books later, I'm finally writing a book devoted solely to the renewing of the mind.

This book isn't a Bible study, but it's not a regular book either. Think of it as a workshop on transformation. Not one of those workshops where you sit for a couple of days, take in a lot of great information, and then go home and forget it.

No, this is a hands-on workshop. Where you focus on one area of your life—something you'd really like to change—and learn how to go to God for help with it.

I'm going to ask you to take on a project. Something you've been trying to change forever with no results. It could be a habit or emotion that hurts your relationship with others. It could be a sin that distances you from God. Or maybe something that just plain makes you miserable.

As you consider different projects, think back to the last time you made New Year's resolutions. What did you want to change? What did you think you'd never be able to change? Since you don't have to rely on your own strength, the sky is the limit for what you can work on.

We'll explore possible projects in chapters 2 and 8-11, but first let's take a look at the overall process we'll be going through. With most workshops, the instructor takes you by the hand and walks you through the steps necessary to complete whatever goal you're working on. This isn't one of those workshops.

Instead, you'll be taking God's hand and going to Him for help with your project. I'm just another person in the class, still working on my own projects.

If you page through the book, you'll notice that the last half is full of Bible verses and questions. In chapters 5 and 6 you'll find practical everyday examples of how to use those questions and Bible verses to go to God for help with your project.

We'll look at the biblical model of transformation in chapters 3 and 12, and we'll look at the renewing of the mind in chapter 4: what it is, why it works, and how to do it on a practical, day-by-day basis. In Chapter 7 we'll look at truth journaling, which is a practical application of 2 Corinthians 10:3-5.

I hope you're getting excited. Not only about changing something you've been wanting to change forever, but also about going to God for help with it. Philippians 4:13 says, "I can do all things through Him who strengthens me." God can help you accomplish your goal, and He tells us how to do that in His Word. We'll talk more about what that will look like in later chapters, but first let's talk about your project.

CHAPTER 2

The Renewing of the Mind Project

IMAGINE THAT YOU'RE standing in the living room of a 50's era ranch-style house. Puke green carpet on the floors. Low ceilings. Outdated light fixtures. Cobwebs hanging from the curtains. And everywhere you look it's dark. Not a drop of light anywhere.

You're standing there with a stack of papers in your hand. The ones you just signed at the bank. The house is yours, and now it's your job to make it a home. There's just one little problem: You know nothing about home improvement and you can't afford to hire a professional.

What would you do?

Would you sit down and cry? Panic? Forget you ever bought the house and head for the nearest donut shop? Or would you pick up a crowbar and get to work?

The renewing of the mind is like fixing up a rickety, old house. The cobwebs are the lies we believe about life and people. The darkness comes from not looking at life through the light of the Word. The shag carpet that runs through the house is like a single lie that affects all areas of our lives: Life should be easy, for example. Or I deserve the good life.

Our job is to open up the windows and let the light of God's Word in *so it can transform us.* That's different than opening the drapes and plopping down on the couch with a good book. But too often that's what we do as Christians.

We make a few obvious changes—get rid of those glaring things that make us look *really* bad—and then we look around and say, "I think that's good enough." With a sigh of relief, we plop back in our church pews and stop pursuing transformation, comfortable in our acceptable-in-the-church sins.

God on the other hand wants us to continue working on transformation throughout our lives (Leviticus 11:44, Matthew 5:48, Matthew 5-7, Hebrews 12, Romans 12:1-2). Not so we can earn salvation, but so we can better reflect His nature to a dying world. So we can love others with a sacrificial love. And so we can love Him with all our heart, soul, mind, and strength.

If God wants us to be transformed, we need to be active about it: look around and see what needs to be changed. Seek out our friend the Carpenter and ask Him to help. Keep our self-improvement manual—the Bible—open at all times for consultation. And pick up the crowbar of truth to chip away at that carpet of lies.

If you've ever done a home improvement project, you know it's not an exact science. Instead, it's a messy, time-consuming, and often expensive project that requires a lot of sacrifice.

It's the same with transformation. As we get into the process, don't make the mistake of thinking this is the easy three-step plan to fix up your life. It's not. Instead, it's a way of life. A continual taking off lies and putting on truth in order to break free from our sins, bad habits, and negative emotions so we can love God and others better.

A Renewing of the Mind Project

So how do you start this way of life? Think back to that decrepit old house we were just talking about. Could you fix that house up in a day? Of course not. If we wanted to fix it up, we wouldn't put "Fix up house" on our list. Instead, we'd choose one room, or even a portion of a room. We'd start with one project and go from there.

We can do the same thing with our spiritual life. God doesn't expect us to have a perfect house pronto the minute we become Christians. He knows the sorry state we're in. That's why He sent Jesus to die on the cross.

So when we start working on these renewing of the mind projects, we're not starting from a point of having to measure up to be acceptable to God.

We're starting from a point of *already* being accepted by God if we're His children through faith (Ephesians 2:4-9). This gives us a secure foundation. We can rest in His love and walk hand in hand with Him, working on this project together.

So let's take a closer look at these projects. Pretend you're back in that forlorn living room of the house you just purchased. Only this time it's not a house. It's you. As you look around, you probably see all kinds of things that need to be changed. But you'll also see some things you like. Let's begin by looking at some of those things.

Try to come up with at least seven of your strengths and list them below. Here are some examples: friendly, loyal, faithful, self-controlled, kind, generous, non-judgmental, willing to serve, patient, loving, joyful, hard-working, discerning, steadfast, accepting, etc.

Your Strengths

1.

2.

3.

4.

5.

6.

7.

How did you do? I asked you to list your strengths first because it's so easy to focus on our weaknesses and get discouraged. God has blessed you with strengths, and He's probably already helped you overcome some weaknesses. But that doesn't mean He's finished with you.

He sees things right now in your life that He'd like to change. Not because He's a demanding perfectionist who's disgusted with you. But because He's a loving Father who cares about you and also about the people you interact with each day.

So as you look at your weaknesses, look at them from the comfort and safety of your Father's arms, knowing that He's looking at them with you, but through eyes of grace and love and a desire to help.

Also remember that He knows what you're going through. He's not a high priest who's never experienced the things you have. He's experienced every temptation. He *knows* how hard it is to live life down here, and He wants to help (Hebrews 4:15-16).

Are you ready to grab hold of His hand and look at some of those "rooms" in your life that might need a remodel? Go ahead and answer the questions below to get some ideas of a project you might like to work on.

Exploring Your Options

1. What areas of your life cause you the most stress?

2. Why do they stress you out?

3. Circle the negative emotions and attitudes you've struggled with lately: worry, fear, stress, grief, sadness, despair, fear of failure,

fear of what people think, anger, annoyance, frustration, self-condemnation, self-pity, insecurity, perfectionism, discontentment, envy, pride, judgment, a critical spirit, anxiety. Which three have you been struggling with the most?

4. What habits and sins have you been struggling with lately?

5. Can you think of any good habits you'd like to develop?

6. Think of your family, friends, and others. What habits and negative emotions get in the way of loving them well?

7. Think of your relationship with God. Which of your habits and negative emotions most interfere with your relationship with Him? Are there any habits you could develop that would improve your relationship?

8. Look back over your answers to the first seven questions. If you could set three goals for the year and be guaranteed you could reach them (which is of course impossible), which goals would you choose?

9. Why would you choose those goals?

10. Which three goals do you think God would choose, and why would He choose them?

11. Look over your answers to the preceding questions and list two or three possible projects you could work on as you go through this book.

As you go through the next few chapters, keep those possible projects at the back of your mind. We'll narrow the focus down to one project in chapter eight, but before we do that, let's take a look at the biblical process of transformation.

CHAPTER 3

Just Say "No" to Sin?

OULDN'T IT BE nice if we could just say a little prayer—*Please take away this sin, God*—then go to sleep and wake up the next day without that sin in our lives? Unfortunately, God doesn't usually work that way! Instead, He asks us to get involved in our own transformation.

To understand our role in the transformation process, let's begin by looking at an Old Testament story: Jericho. Remember that story? God wanted to deliver Jericho into the hands of the Israelites, but He didn't hand it over on a platter.

Instead, He gave the Israelites a job: Walk around the city once a day for six days. Then walk around it seven times on the seventh day. Then give a big old shout, and the walls will fall down (Joshua 6).

Think about that for a minute. What would you have thought if you were one of the Israelites? Would you have been a bit skeptical? Would you have been wondering why God doesn't just make the walls fall down right away with no effort on your part? Or would you have been itching to fight with man-made weapons?

Sometimes we're so used to doing things one way, that we have a hard time thinking of doing them another way—especially when that other way doesn't make sense to us. But misgivings or not, the Israelites did what God asked and the walls of Jericho fell.

No one can deny that God was the one who caused the walls to fall. But here's my question: Do you think God would have destroyed the walls of Jericho if the Israelites had refused to walk and shout?

I don't think so. God *wanted* to give the Israelites victory, but He wasn't going to do it without their involvement.

It's the same with us and transformation. God wants to give us victory over our sins, controlling habits, and negative emotions, and He could do it in the blink of an eye. But He rarely does. Instead, He expects us to be involved in our own transformation, and He doesn't usually change us unless we get involved.

The question is, what *is* our role in transformation? In recent years the church has muddied the waters of this issue because it gives us advice that requires no effort on our parts. Here are just a few of the things I've been hearing lately on transformation:

1. Just say no to sin.

2. Claim the victory that has already been won.

3. Rely on grace.

4. Stop striving.

5. Let go and let God.

6. Get an accountability partner.

7. Be authentic. Share your struggles with others.

If you look at that list, you'll see some great things on it. It's true that it does no good to strive in our own strength. It's true that we have to rely on God's grace. It's true that it helps to share our struggles with others.

It's true that accountability helps. And it's true that the ultimate victory has already been won: Jesus conquered sin through His death and resurrection, and we're already new creatures if we're His children through faith (2 Corinthians 5:15-21, Romans 6:4-11).

But if you look at what the Bible says about our role in the sanctification process, you'll find a completely different list than the one I just mentioned. Here are seven things the Bible tells us to do *after* we're saved, if we want to be transformed:

1. Renew your mind (Romans 12:2).

2. Hide God's word in your heart (Psalm 119:11).

3. Fight with spiritual weapons (Ephesians 6:10-18).

4. Take your thoughts captive to the truth (2 Corinthians 10:3-5).

5. Abide in Jesus (John 15:1-5).

6. Abide in God's Word (John 8:31-32).

7. Walk by the Spirit (Galatians 5:16-25).

Do you see what an active role God asks us to play in the transformation process? The first list doesn't require any effort on our part, and the second list requires all kinds of effort. But there's a problem: The word *effort* is often seen as a no-no in the church today. We mistakenly think that if we talk about effort, suddenly we're not believing in salvation by grace through faith, and we're going all legalistic.

Nothing could be further from the truth. Think back to Jericho. God was the one who broke those walls down, not the Israelites. But He told them, you *have* to walk if you want the walls to fall down.

We see this sort of thing happening throughout Scripture. Naaman had to dip in the water seven times to be healed (2 Kings 5). The rich young ruler had to give up everything to be Jesus's disciple (Matthew 19:16-22). And James told us that faith without works is dead (James 2:14-26).

The truth is, God expects us to put effort into our faith. He doesn't demand perfection, but He does demand sacrifice (Ephesians 2:8, Matthew 16:24-26, 19:16-22). When we hear the word sacrifice, we automatically think of doing big things. Things like becoming a missionary or going door-to-door witnessing.

But sacrificing as a Christian is about more than just becoming a missionary or witnessing. It's about laying down our lives to love God and others well. The more we stay stuck in our sins and negative emotions like worry, anger, and insecurity, the harder it is to do that. So God asks us to work on getting rid of those things. He wants us to put effort into our own transformation (Hebrews 12:1-14).

But what kind of effort is expected of us? It's no use just trying to get rid of our sin in our own strength. We can't do that anymore than the Israelites could have pushed down the walls of Jericho.

No, we need to put effort into the things God asks us to do—that list I mentioned earlier: abiding in the Word, renewing our minds, fighting with spiritual weapons, taking our thoughts captive, and walking in the Spirit.

As we do what He asks us to do, He'll begin to transform us. Do you see how similar it is to the Israelites' experience in Jericho? He's the One doing the work, but He rarely does it unless we walk alongside Him.

So what does that look like on a practical level? That's what we'll be talking about in the rest of this book. But before we get to that practical section, I want to talk about the renewing of the mind since that's the main focus of this book.

What is the renewing of the mind? How do you do it? Why is it so important? That's what we'll talk about in the next chapter.

CHAPTER 4

How to Renew Your Mind

IF SOMEONE TOLD you to have a quiet time, you'd know what to do: read your Bible and pray. But what if they told you to renew your mind? Would you know what they wanted? Probably not. The renewing of the mind doesn't have a clear protocol like a quiet time has. Maybe that's because it's so messy.

With a quiet time, you know you've done it when you've "read your Bible and prayed." With the renewing of the mind, you know you've done it when you're seeing life—and more specifically, your current situation—from a biblical perspective.

The renewing of the mind, like a home improvement project, is a taking off and a putting on. You take off the old self. You put on the new self. You take off the lies. You put on the truth. You take off a cultural perspective. You put on a biblical perspective. You take off what you learned growing up. You put on what you learned in the Bible.

The renewing of the mind is an active time of fellowship with God:

discussing life with Him, listening to Him, telling Him what you think about your current situation, and asking Him what He thinks.

One of the ways we find out what He thinks is through reading His Word. But the renewing of the mind is more than just reading the Word. It's mulling over the Word, meditating on the Word, memorizing the Word, and allowing the Word to transform us.

When we read the Bible, we're putting on truth. But unless we interact with the Bible—unless we use it to change the way we think about life—we're not doing the taking off part that Paul talks about in Ephesians 4:22-24. Let's take a look at that passage:

> *That in reference to your former manner of life, you lay aside the old self, which is being corrupted in accordance with the lusts of deceit, and that you be renewed in the spirit of your mind, and put on the new self, which in the likeness of God has been created in righteousness and holiness of the truth.*

In this passage Paul tells us to do three things: lay aside the old self, be renewed in the spirit of our minds, and put on the new self. He then goes on to tell us what's corrupting the old self: the lusts of deceit.

In order to understand that phrase, we need to take a look at how the Greeks handled the possessive noun. If I lived in Jesus's day, I wouldn't say, "This is my husband's coat." I'd say, "This is the coat of my husband." And instead of saying, "This is God's word," I'd say, "This is the word of God." The word belongs to God and comes from God. It's God's word.

So if we look at the phrase "lusts of deceit" in Ephesians 4:22, the lusts that corrupt us come from the lies (deceit) we believe about life, our habits, others, ourselves, and even God. We could show the relationship with the following diagram:

Lies (Deceit) ⇨ Intense Desires (Lusts) ⇨ Old Self Actions (Corruption)

We see this relationship between lies and lust at work since the beginning of time. In Genesis 3:1-7 Satan tempts Eve with lies. He says, "Eve,

Eve, it's just a little piece of fruit. You're not going to *die* just from eating a little piece of fruit. And besides, if you eat this, you'll know the difference between good and evil. How could that not be a good thing, Eve?"

By the time Satan is through with her, Eve is thinking, *Of course I'm going to eat it! Give me that fruit!!!* Believing Satan's lies created an intense desire in her to eat the forbidden fruit and she ate it. If you look back at Ephesians 4:22, Eve was corrupted in accordance with the lusts of deceit.

But what if Eve had taken the time to go to God *before* eating the fruit and be renewed in the spirit of her mind (Ephesians 4:23)? What if she had said, "Wait a minute, Satan, let me talk to God about this first even though it seems like a no-brainer, that of course I should eat the fruit."

If she had taken the time to do that, God could have given her *His* argument for not eating the fruit. He would have reminded her of the consequences. He would have reminded her of the sweet fellowship they shared and how that fellowship would be broken if she disobeyed Him. He would have reminded her of how He had taken care of her in the past and how she could trust Him in the present, even if she didn't understand His reason for not eating the fruit.

After soaking in God's presence and looking at the temptation from *His* perspective, Eve would have actually wanted to obey Him. And that would have given her the strength to say no to Satan.

We can relate to Eve. When we're in the midst of temptation, everything within us is screaming at us to just give in and do it! We're believing lies right and left—so many lies that there's no way we can say no to temptation in our own strength.

We desperately need to go to God for help so we can see the situation from His perspective. Because when we see it from His point of view, we'll actually *want* to obey Him.

The truth is, Satan and the lies of this world are so convincing that unless we go to God again and again to discuss life with Him, we won't have much of a chance of living the way He asks us to live. If we want to be victorious over our habits and emotions, we need to take the time to renew our minds.

Habits Example

Let's see how this would play out with a modern day example. Since pornography is such a huge struggle for both men and women, let's take a look at trying to break a porn habit. Here are three lies you might believe if you were struggling with pornography:

1. This isn't hurting anyone.

2. I deserve this since a) my spouse isn't meeting my needs, b) I'm not having sex with my boyfriend/girlfriend (and everyone else is having sex), or c) I'm single and I have needs just like everyone else.

3. This isn't a sin since I'm not having sex.

Do you see how those lies would create an intense desire to look at pornography? Not only would we have a natural curiosity (or a cultivated desire if we'd been doing it for awhile), we'd also have all those lies telling us it's okay to do it. Those lies would turn a little desire into a big desire because all of a sudden, our behavior would be justified.

If we wanted to break free from pornography (or avoid a porn habit), we'd have two options: Either we could muster up all of our self control and "just say no to sin," or we could take the time to renew our minds every time we felt like giving in to temptation. In other words, take the time to see pornography from God's perspective.

That first option sounds spiritual, but it doesn't work. Here's why: because we're trying to say no in our own strength, and we're not taking advantage of the spiritual weapons God has given us to use in moments of temptation. One of those spiritual weapons is truth. Paul talks about it in Ephesians 6:14-17 and again in 2 Corinthians 10:3-5 when he says,

For though we walk in the flesh, we do not war according to the flesh, for the weapons of our warfare are not of the flesh, but divinely powerful for the destruction of fortresses. We are destroying speculations and every lofty thing raised up against

the knowledge of God, and we are taking every thought captive to the obedience of Christ.

Let's try out Paul's advice and take every thought captive to the obedience of Christ. We'll look at the thoughts that fuel a porn habit and see what Jesus would have to say about each thought.

Thought #1:
This isn't hurting anyone.

Would Jesus agree that this isn't hurting anyone? I don't think so. Pornography as an industry hurts all kinds of people. Just think of all the kids who have been molested by people whose passions were fueled by pornography, or the women who have been raped for the same reason, or the people who have been photographed against their will.

We would have no way of knowing the story of the person we're looking at on the Internet. We wouldn't know if they were posing against their will. And if they were posing willingly, we wouldn't know what brought them to that point.

Pornography hurts its victims, but it also hurts the people who view it. If we were to get caught up in porn—even if we didn't end up raping or molesting anyone—it would hurt our relationship with God and others. Why? Because aside from the fact that lust is a sin (and sin hurts our relationship with God), pornography would encourage us to think about *our* needs, our wants, and our desires. And God wants us to be thinking about other people (Philippians 2:4-8).

He wouldn't say, "Yes, go ahead, look at those people I love. I made them for your enjoyment. It's not a big deal that you're not married to them and don't even know them." He would never say that. Instead, He'd say, "I love those people you're looking at. I know their life story. I know why they're on the Internet in such a vulnerable state. I know how difficult their lives are. Why are you looking at them as if they were objects to be enjoyed? They're people."

Not too long ago I viewed an innocent looking Twitter profile that was sprinkled with pornographic images. I had a hard time getting those images out of my mind until I remembered that those "images" were real people: people who were living life, going to work, coming home, preparing meals, struggling and hurting, just like the rest of us. I started praying for those women and before long, the images faded and the real people appeared. My struggle was over.

Now granted, it was a ten-minute struggle, not a lifetime habit. But the principle remains no matter how long we've been struggling with a habit: We are transformed by the renewing of the mind. Not by self-control. Not by willpower. Not by brute strength.

Self-control is a fruit of the Spirit (Galatians 5:22-23). We obtain it by walking through life with God (Galatians 5:16-25, John 15:4-5), not by frantically trying to drum it up in a tempting situation. Let's look at that second thought.

Thought #2:

I deserve this since a) my spouse isn't meeting my needs, b) I'm not having sex with my boyfriend or girlfriend (and everyone else is having sex), or c) I'm single and I have needs just like everyone else.

This is a common justification for pornography, but is it true? Would Jesus say, "You poor thing, I can see how deprived you are. Of course you deserve a little pornography"? Of course not! Jesus was all about *giving up* rights to love people well. Not about hanging on to them so we can be happy. He said things like, "Whoever wants to be my disciple must deny themselves and take up their cross and follow me" (Matthew 16:24).

When we read that verse we often think of big things, things like being persecuted for our faith. But the truth is, we have all kinds of opportunities to deny ourselves and take up our cross for Him. One of the ways we do that is by holding our habits with open hands, willing to give them up to love God and others well.

Thought #3:
This isn't a sin since I'm not having sex.

So often in Christianity we focus on the behavior and ignore the heart. So as long as we're not actually having sex outside of marriage, we think it's okay to do everything else up to that point. All we need to do is read the Sermon on the Mount in Matthew 5-7 to see that Jesus is just as concerned with our hearts as He is with our behavior. And one of the things He says in the Sermon on the Mount is, "Do not lust" (Matthew 5:27-29).

So the minute you feel that intense desire rising up for someone besides your spouse, whether it's viewing pornography, watching a television commercial, or making out with a boyfriend or girlfriend, you've slipped over into the sin category.

Another way to tell if we've slipped over into the sin category is to check our thoughts and motives: Do we have that person's best interest at heart (Philippians 2:3-4), or are we more focused on our own interests? Are we viewing them as people or objects? And last but not least, if Jesus were with us, would He be happy with our thoughts? If the answer is no, then it's time to renew our minds so we can love others with a sincere heart (1 Peter 1:22).

Truth Changes Desires

Are you beginning to see how God uses truth to transform us? In that last example, taking the time to renew our minds would affect both our emotions and our ability to say no to our habit. It would take away the negative emotion of lust, and it would make us not even *want* to give into temptation. This isn't surprising because truth changes both desires and behavior.

Paul talks about that in Ephesians 4:24 when he tells us to put on the new self, which has been created in righteousness and holiness of the truth. Remember how they wrote possessive nouns in the Greek? The righteousness and holiness come from and belong to the truth. We can see the relationship with the following diagram:

Truth ⇨ Right Desires or a Lack of Intense Wrong Desires ⇨ Holiness (New Self)

We saw this diagram played out in the pornography example, and we saw how it could have played out with Eve if she had taken the time to talk to God before eating the fruit. The truth is, when we see life, people, and our habits from God's perspective, our feelings and desires change. We no longer want to sin. We actually *want* to do the right thing. Truth leads to holy, new-self behavior.

Jesus emphasized this point in His prayer for the disciples before He went to the cross. Listen to His prayer in John 17:17: *Sanctify them in the truth. Your Word is truth.* Truth is necessary for sanctification. It changes our desires, and it gives us the strength to do what God asks us to do.

A Taking Off, A Putting On

When we renew our minds, we're taking off lies and putting on truth. There are many ways to do this, but we'll talk about four different ways in this book: Scripture meditation, Scripture prayer, conversations with God using the questions in this book, and truth journaling. If you'd like more ideas of different ways to renew your mind, look at the Renewing of the Mind Tools tab at my blog.

As you start out on your renewing of the mind project, try to remember how powerful the truth is. Jesus tells us in John 8:32 that the truth will set us free. Paul tells us in 2 Timothy 3:16 that all Scripture is inspired by God and profitable for teaching, reproof, correction, and training in righteousness.

In the last section of this book I've included some Bible verses to serve as a jumping off point to go to the Word for help with your habits and emotions. Because the Bible is so vital to the successful completion of your project, let's begin by taking a look at how you can use the Bible verses to renew your mind.

CHAPTER 5

4 Ways to Use the Bible Verses

W E'VE TALKED ABOUT what the renewing of the mind looks like on a conceptual level: a taking off and a putting on. But how do you do that in real life? In the next few chapters we'll look at some practical ways to renew your mind.

Since the renewing of the mind is so dependent on Scripture, let's begin by looking at how to use the Bible to renew your mind. We'll look at four different renewing of the mind tools in this chapter: 1) Scripture memorization 2) Scripture meditation 3) Scripture as a weapon 4) Scripture prayers.

Scripture Memorization

Psalm 119:11 says, "I have hidden your word in my heart that I might not sin against you" (NIV). When we take the time to memorize Scripture, we have those Bible verses always available to us: when we're lying in bed at night fretting, when we're having a difficult conversation with a friend, when we're surrounded by opportunities to practice that habit we're trying to break, and when we're smack dab in the middle of temptation, struggling to say "no" to sin.

If you look through the last section of this book—the questions and Bible verses section—you'll find all kinds of helpful Bible verses. Write a few of them on index cards and then carry them around with you until you have them memorized. Many of these verses are also available on the I Deserve a Donut app.

You could also download a Bible memory app to help you memorize other helpful Bible verses. Or just take your index cards along with you while you're exercising, brushing your teeth, taking the dog for a walk, cooking, or any other time you have available (I'm preaching to myself here). If you have a hard time memorizing, try writing and rewriting the verses from memory. It may also help to circle keywords in the verse to jog your memory.

Scripture Meditation

Another way to use the Bible verses is to meditate on them. Scripture meditation goes beyond just reading the Bible verse to really spending some time thinking about it. Here are a few questions you could ask when you're meditating:

1. What does this verse mean?

2. Is this the way I usually think about life?

3. If not, why don't I think about life this way?

4. Am I believing any lies?

5. How does the truth of this verse speak to the lies I'm believing?

6. What is God really saying here?

7. How will this verse affect my life?

I sometimes like to break verses into little pieces and think of the pieces one at a time. Here's an example: Let's say I'm trying to break the habit of spending too much time on Facebook. 1 Corinthians 6:12 says, "All things are lawful for me, but not all things are profitable. All things are lawful for me, but I will not be mastered by anything." Here's how I might meditate on 1 Corinthians 6:12:

> *Hmm, profitable, what does that mean? Oh, I know, profitable means that it's good for me. I'm getting a benefit out of it. Kind of like a business. There are revenues and expenses and the profit is what you get when you subtract the expenses from the revenues.*
>
> *What are the benefits (revenues) of Facebook? Well, it's fun. It's a good way to stay connected. I guess that's about it. What are the expenses? Well, it takes up far too much of my time. In some ways it's not all that fun because it's not relaxing or peaceful. And it also keeps me from doing other things I should be doing. Plus it controls me. I have a hard time staying away from it. That's not good.*
>
> *Let me read that verse again: All things are lawful for me—that's true of Facebook because it's not a sin—but not all things are profitable. You know what? This is true. My current use of Facebook isn't profitable. The expenses exceed the revenues. I wonder if I should just limit Facebook, or would it be better to get rid of it completely for a month or two?*

At this point I would probably take a break to talk to God about my Facebook habit and then move on to the second part of the verse: *All things are lawful for me, but I will not be mastered by anything.* Here's an example of how I might meditate on the second half of the verse:

> *Is Facebook mastering me? Do I control Facebook, or does it control me? I'm afraid it controls me. I don't want to be mastered by Facebook. What will I need to do so that I won't be mastered by it? Well, I probably need to follow my boundaries (pp. 60-61) and renew my mind every time I break them. Plus maybe it would be helpful to think of some practical things I could do to reduce the temptation. Maybe I should think about getting a friend to hold me accountable to both my boundaries and renewing my mind when I break them.*

Do you see how much more I would get out of this verse if I were to spend some time meditating on it, rather than just reading it? A casual read-through of the Bible isn't necessarily a renewing of the mind experience. In order for it to be a renewing of the mind experience, we need to be interacting with God's Word. Thinking about it and allowing it to change the way we view life.

Scripture as a Spiritual Weapon

Have you ever struggled with the same sin over and over again—and asked God to take away the desire over and over again—and nothing seemed to happen? No words from God? No change in your sin? No change in your desires?

Often we think we just need to ask God to take away our sinful thoughts and desires, and He'll do it. So we ask away and then get discouraged when nothing happens. Interestingly, Jesus didn't use this approach. Remember when Satan was tempting Him in the desert? Not once did Jesus say, "Lord, please help me say no to temptation!" or "Lord, please take away my desire!"

Instead, every time Satan tempted Him, Jesus answered with Scripture. Jesus was modeling Ephesians 6:17 for us. He was engaging in spiritual warfare. Using the sword of the spirit—the word of God—to fight temptation.

If *Jesus* needed Scripture to fight temptation, how much more so do we need it! This is where that Scripture memorization comes in handy. If you've taken the time to memorize a few Bible verses, you can pull them out in the midst of temptation to fight Satan's lies with God's truth.

Here's an example: Let's say you're doing a project on judgment and you've made a commitment to renew your mind every time you catch yourself being judgmental. You're sitting in church listening to the sermon when all of a sudden you notice that person up in the front row of the church. The one who drives you crazy.

You remember what she did and said last week, and before you know it, you've stopped listening to the sermon, and you're instead thinking about what a terrible person she is. You remember your commitment, so you take a break and meditate on the Bible verses for judgment that you've hopefully already memorized to use in situations like this.

Here's another example. Let's say you're working on a renewing of the mind project to break free from the control of food. You're going through the line at the church potluck, and you're having a hard time putting a reasonable amount on your plate. As you go through the line, you could keep repeating Romans 13:14 to yourself: *But put on the Lord Jesus Christ, and make no provision for the flesh in regard to its lusts.*

If you take the time to memorize some Bible verses, you'll find all kinds of opportunities to use them as weapons in the midst of temptation. If you haven't memorized them, you can still pull out your Bible or your index cards or your book or your app. Scripture is powerful. We just need to remember to take advantage of its power!

Scripture Prayers

I first read about Scripture prayer in Beth Moore's book, *Praying God's Word.* Praying Scripture is a powerful way to renew our minds because it helps us look at life from God's perspective. There are two different ways to pray Scripture. First, you can just alter the wording a bit and pray the Scripture right back to God. Second, you can use the passage as a springboard for a conversation with God.

Here's an example of how to use Scripture prayers in your renewing of the mind project: Let's say you're working on a worry project, and you've made a commitment to renew your mind every time you worry about a family member.

Your spouse (or son or dad) is late coming home from a hike, and you've been trying to get ahold of him for the last few hours with no success. You're worried sick, so you decided to follow through on your commitment to renew your mind. Here's a prayer that would *not* renew your mind:

> *Lord, where is Mark? I can't believe he's not home yet. He should have been here hours ago. What happened to him? I wonder if he broke his leg. I bet he's lying up on the mountain someplace and can't move! And it's supposed to get down to 20 degrees tonight! He'll never make it, Lord. He'll die of hypothermia! What am I going to do? I'll never make it without him. Life will*

be miserable. I wonder if his parents will come for his funeral?
Lord, will you please let him come home safely?

Do you think that prayer would help us stop worrying about Mark? I doubt it! Instead it just rehearsed our belief that Mark is probably going to die—or maybe he's already dead—and that life will be terrible without him.

A renewing of the mind prayer would help us remember that life is about God, that He's all powerful, and that we can trust Him no matter what happens…even if Mark ends up dying. Here's an example of a Scripture prayer that would renew our minds based on Revelations 22:13, Matthew 10:30, and Romans 8:28:

> *Oh Father, will you please take care of Mark for me? You know Him so well that the very hairs on his head are numbered. So of course you know exactly where he is right now. Please keep Him safe for me. You are the Alpha and the Omega, the First and the Last, the Beginning and the End. You can do anything. Thank you for that, Lord. And thank you for who you are in the midst of this trial. Thank you for how you've helped me in the past. And thank you that I can trust you no matter what happens. Lord, please help me to hold Mark with open hands. Help me remember that life is about you. Thank you, Lord. I place Mark in your hands.*

Do you see how much more helpful this prayer would be than our first prayer? Not only would it help us to stop worrying, it would also remind us that life is about God, not Mark. So that even if something were to happen to Mark, we'd still be okay.

It's important to note that all of this renewing of the mind is done in addition to whatever else we decide to do. In this situation we could drive to the trailhead to see if Mark's car is there, or we could start hiking up the trail to see if we can find him or call in Search and Rescue at some point if he doesn't show up.

So it's not that we just sit back and go to God for help to let go of our negative emotions. We also ask Him for wisdom and look for practical ways to improve a situation, no matter what emotion we're dealing with. So if I were working on a discontentment project, I would renew my mind every time I was discontent, but I would also work on practical solutions to make my life better, as long as those practical solutions would be okay with God.

If you haven't tried praying Scripture yet, I hope you'll give it a try. Just go to the questions and Bible verses that correspond to your emotion or temptation and use the Bible verses to have a conversation with God about the situation. It may also be helpful to write these prayers in your journal.

Another way to have a conversation with God is to use the questions in this book as a jumping off point to talk to Him about your habits and emotions. Let's take a look at those next.

CHAPTER 6

Conversations With God

D O YOU EVER wish you could just visit with Jesus over a cup of coffee? See what He thinks about your problems? Ask Him for advice? Although that would be wonderful, on this earth we have to content ourselves with talking to Him through prayer.

That's not a bad thing though, because prayer at its core is simply a back and forth conversation between God and us. The questions in the last section of this book will help you have those conversations with God about life.

If you're not familiar with the questions, take a minute to look at the Table of Contents. You'll see three sets of questions and Bible verses: Starting a Habit (or Pursuing a Goal), Stopping a Habit, and Emotions. You can use these questions to renew your mind whenever you're struggling with your habit or emotions.

Just read through the list in the Table of Contents and choose a set of questions that seems to best fit your current situation. Then use those questions to have a conversation with God about your situation.

What I usually do is go through a few questions, take a break and visit with God a bit, and then go back to the questions again. The questions are just there for a structure. Something to get you started in visiting with God about your problems.

Use a Variety of Questions

Usually there are several sets of questions you can use each time you renew your mind. Try to use a variety, as each set of questions will bring up new topics of conversation. Here's an example: Let's say you're working on a renewing of the mind project for worry, and you've made a commitment to renew your mind every time you're worried.

You're currently in the middle of the wilderness, huddled in a flimsy tent, listening to the wind roar and the thunder boom, and wondering whether you're more likely to die by a lightening strike or a tree falling on your tent. You can't help but worry, so you decide to follow through on your commitment to renew your mind.

The worry questions are an obvious choice, but those aren't the only questions you could use. Look for other sets as well.

For example, you may be kicking yourself for going on the trip in the first place. Or you may be annoyed with your friend who talked you into the trip. Or you may be afraid that your hiking partners will think you're a baby for being so scared. If you're feeling that way, you could use the regret, annoyance, or insecurity/feeling rejected and condemned questions to renew your mind, as well as the worry questions.

Here's another example. Let's say you're annoyed with a family member. You work through the anger questions—the obvious choice—but you're still mad. You may need to work through more than one set of questions to get to the root of the problem and experience peace. The pride and judgment questions would also be helpful, as well as the insecurity, regret, or greed/lust questions, depending on why you're annoyed.

If you have a hard time deciding which questions to use, just start at the beginning and go through one or two sets a day. No matter what questions you use, you can usually think of some way to apply them to your current project. Also, don't be afraid to skip back and forth between the categories. If you're trying to break a habit, for example, look for questions in the emotions and starting a habit categories, as well as the stopping a habit category.

Remember That God Already Loves You

As you go through the questions, remember that our ultimate goal is to love God and others well—not to become perfect people so God and others will love us well. The truth is, God already loves and accepts us if we're His children through faith (Ephesians 2:8-9). He has cleansed us with His blood, and clothed us in His righteousness. He doesn't demand perfection. And if others are going to love and accept us, they'll have to love and accept the imperfect us since the perfect version won't be available until heaven.

The more we look at our renewing of the mind projects as a time to visit with God about life, the more we'll enjoy the experience. God *loves* us and He wants to help us with our problems. What an incredible blessing that is. The renewing of the mind is a gift. An opportunity to spend time talking over life with the One we love. Let's see what one of those conversations might look like.

Pretend that you've struggled with insecurity all your life (most of us won't have to pretend), and you've decided to work on insecurity for your renewing of the mind project. You've made a commitment to renew your mind every time you feel insecure in a social setting, and you've just come home from a new exercise class, where you felt like a total loser. The class was filled with buff men and skinny women, and you are neither. You had a hard time reaching out to people because you felt like everyone was judging you.

Here are a few sets of questions you could use to have a conversation with God about the experience: insecurity/feeling inadequate, insecurity/feeling rejected or condemned, insecurity/social situations, greed/lust (what you want is to be skinny or buff), and possibly envy, depending on how you were feeling about the others in the class. Let's do the insecurity/

feeling inadequate questions together. I'll show you how I would answer the questions if I were the person in this example:

Insecurity: Feeling Inadequate

Why do you think you're inadequate?

Because I'm overweight, out of shape, and not that good looking.

What do you think you have to do or have to be acceptable?

Lose weight and get in shape for starters. And looking good would be nice too if I could make it happen.

Are you capable of making that happen right now?

No. I might be able to spend a little more time on my looks and make myself look better, but I can't lose weight and get in shape overnight.

What do you look like when you see yourself through the eyes of the world and/or the eyes of your own expectations?

A loser!!

Is that how God sees you?

This is where I start breathing my first sigh of relief. Because this is the question that will make me start realizing, *Oh, that's right. I'm believing a lie. I'm not a loser just because the world thinks I'm a loser.* (Not to mention the fact that I don't really know what the people in the class are thinking. I might just be imagining things.) Here's how I would answer this question:

No.

Who are you in God's eyes, and how does He feel about you? (Look at the insecurity/feeling inadequate verses for ideas.)

In God's eyes, I am beautifully and wonderfully made. He sees me as His bride, His beloved child, His work of art! I am a chosen race, a royal priesthood, a holy nation. He loves me in my "as is" condition. He loves me with an everlasting love. And He rejoices over me with shouts of joy. (Psalm 139:13-15, Isaiah 62:4-5, Jeremiah 31:3-4, 20, Ephesians 2:10, 1 Peter 2:9, Romans 5:8, Zephaniah 3:17)

I would be starting to feel pretty good here after going through all those Bible verses.

How is God's view of you different than your own view or the world's view?

God sees the real me, the inside me. The world sees the outside me. The world cares about looks, success, popularity, etc. God cares about character. God sees me through eyes of grace. The world—at least the one in my mind—sees me through eyes of condemnation. Or maybe they don't, and I just think they do.

This would make me think, *Oh, maybe I should do the self-condemnation or the feeling rejected and condemned questions.*

If the Living God, King of the Universe, says you're acceptable, does anyone else, including you, have the right to say you're unacceptable?

This question will start getting my heart rate up. I'll start thinking, *Hey!! I don't need to measure up to these cultural standards! That's ridiculous!!!* I'll answer the questions with a resounding, *No!! I'm acceptable no matter what anyone thinks!*

Is God's love enough to satisfy you even if you're not the person you want to be?

This question makes me stop and think, *Am I caring too much about what everyone in the class thinks? Probably.* I would probably take a break here to talk with God about this. When I finished, I would go back to the questions and answer this one with a resounding, *Yes, He's enough!*

What can you thank God for in this situation?

At this point, I'd probably just start praying and thanking God for everything I could think of to thank Him for, including who He is in the midst of this trial. Here's what that might look like:

Thank you, God, that you love me in my "as is" condition. Thank you that I don't need to measure up to gain your acceptance. Thank you that you care more about my insides than my outsides. Thank you that I don't have to be perfect to be acceptable. Thank you that you're enough. That if everyone in the world were to stand up in unison and shout, "You're a loser!!!!" that you would look at me with love in your eyes and say, "No, she's not." I love you, Lord. I love who you are. I love how you love. I love everything about you. I am blessed!! Thank you!

Do you see why I'd start feeling more secure as I went through the questions? The questions would help me see life from God's perspective. And life always looks better when we look at it from His perspective.

The questions would also help me realize that the people at the gym are just regular people and that it's okay if they don't like me since God loves me. Oddly, this would help me actually want to reach out to them.

Do you remember how I said different sets of questions would bring up different conversations? This conversation mostly focused on how I feel about myself and who I am in God's eyes. If I had done the feeling condemned questions, I would have looked at the question, "Are these people really condemning me?" I would probably have realized that, no, most of them aren't. I'm just thinking they are.

If I had looked at the insecurity/social situations or the envy questions, I would have had an opportunity to look at my own feelings for the people in the class and how God wanted me to feel towards them. So it helps to have different conversations about the same situation if you're working on breaking free from an emotion such as insecurity.

An Engaged Mind

As you go through the questions, remember that just reading them won't do a thing for you, nor will giving a quick response. In order to be a renewing of the mind experience, your mind will have to be actively engaged in taking off lies, putting on truth, and trying to see life from God's perspective.

If you find yourself having a hard time concentrating, try writing the answers out in your journal. Then take breaks to talk to God. I also take breaks to repent and ask forgiveness whenever I realize I've been having a sinful attitude.

Another thing I sometimes do is to just do the questions in my mind, but visit with God about each question so it's more of an ongoing conversation. Try both ways to see if one way is more helpful than another.

Intimacy with God

As you have those conversations with God, remember that He's a loving Father who wants to help you, not a perfectionist parent who wants to condemn you. If you think of all the times in the Bible when God is mad at people, they're all times when the people are either saying they have no sin or sitting comfortably in their sin or idolatry, refusing to do anything about it. He doesn't get mad at people who are recognizing their sin, repenting of it, and going to Him for help with it.

Remember also that Jesus has been in your shoes. He's struggled with every temptation you have (Hebrews 4:15). He understands what you're going through and is perfectly suited to help you work through your problems. And finally, remember that the Holy Spirit is your teacher (John 14:26), and He wants to give you advice.

In a sense, the renewing of the mind is like a counseling session with the One who loves you better than you could ever imagine being loved. It's an incredible time of intimate fellowship, but it's also a time of conviction. It often brings me to my knees in repentance as I become aware of my sin.

One of the things I love about the questions and Bible verses is that they provide a path for me to go to God for help with my problems. My prayer is that they will do the same for you.

CHAPTER 7

Truth Journaling

WHEN I WAS young, I had a little diary with a lock and key. I would spill all my secrets onto its crinkly pages and lock it up so no one could read it. I've always enjoyed journaling, but it wasn't until I was forty that God began to change my life with it. That was the year I started truth journaling.

Often people advocate the use of journaling as a way to clear the air: to get all those bad thoughts out of your system so they don't poison you. Truth journaling is different. You're still spilling your thoughts out, but for the purpose of examining them and bringing them captive to the truth. It's a practical application of 2 Corinthians 10:3-5:

> *For though we walk in the flesh, we do not war according to the flesh, for the weapons of our warfare are not of the flesh but divinely powerful for the destruction of fortresses. We are destroying speculations and every lofty thing raised up against*

the knowledge of God, and we are taking every thought captive to the obedience of Christ.

Truth journaling is a great way to renew our minds because it helps us see life from a biblical perspective, but it's also a form of spiritual warfare because we're taking off the lies that the enemy is throwing at us and replacing those lies with the truth of God's Word.

The best way to learn how to truth journal is to just jump in and give it a try. Picture yourself in this situation: You're trying to break your habit, and you just made it through a week of following your boundaries (pp. 60-61). You're starting to feel hopeful that *this* time you might actually be successful at breaking your habit. Then something happens to trip you up, and you have an evening of practicing your habit full force. Can you imagine how you'd feel? Let's try truth journaling about it.

Step One: Spill Out Your Thoughts

Begin by spilling your thoughts onto the pages of your journal. This usually takes me less than a minute. I end up with maybe six or seven sentences. These aren't "Let's see, what am I thinking?" sorts of thoughts. They're gut level thoughts. In fact, you may even know they're untrue as you write them. Here's what I might write in my journal if I had just majorly broken my boundaries:

> *I can't believe I did that. I'm such a failure. I'll never break this habit. I try and try and try and nothing happens. This time is just like all the other times. Why do I even bother? I should just give up.*

Can you see what a jumble my thoughts are? I'm not organizing them first. I'm just spilling them out onto the paper. It took me about 30 seconds.

Step Two: Number your thoughts.

The next thing you do is number each sentence. This will force you to look at each thought, rather than the whole overwhelming situation. This isn't natural. Our tendency is to focus on the big picture.

We come up with a conclusion—I'm such a failure, for example—and then we think of all the dumb things we've ever done that prove that we're a failure. This just solidifies our conclusion that things *really are bad.*

Satan loves that. He wants us to think of life and people—and ourselves—in terms of black and white. Either we're wonderful—or we're terrible. And of course he would prefer terrible since he's the condemner of the saints (Revelations 12:10).

Paul tells us in 2 Corinthians 10:3-5 how to fight Satan's attacks: take each thought captive. Let's do that. Think of each sentence as a thought. If it's a long sentence, you may want to break it up into a couple of thoughts. We'll begin by numbering our sentences:

1. I can't believe I did that. 2. I'm such a failure. 3. I'll never break this habit. 4. I try and try and nothing happens. 5. This time is just like all the other times. 6. Why do I even bother? 7. I should just give up.

Next, we'll look at each sentence—one at a time—to see if it's true or false. If it's true, we'll write true. If it's false—or only half-true—we'll rewrite it so it's all the way true. Satan is the master of the partial truth so we'll often find thoughts that are somewhat true, but not all the way true. Keep your eye out for those thoughts.

Step Three: Write the Truth for Each Lie

Step three is one that will take a little practice: write the truth for each lie. This is difficult for a couple of reasons. First, we don't always recognize lies when we see them. And second, it may take some thinking to figure out the truth.

Sometimes we've believed lies for so long that it's hard to recognize them. That's why it's so important to look at your thoughts one sentence at a time. It's far easier to see the lie in one sentence than it is to see the lies in a whole paragraph. So close your mind to the rest of the paragraph and just focus on that one particular sentence.

For example, if I'm looking at the sentence, "I'm such a failure," in light of the rest of the paragraph, I would say, "Yes, I *am* a failure. Look at how many times I've failed." But if I hold that sentence up to the light of God's

Word, I can see the truth: I'm a beloved child of God who fails at times, and this isn't all that surprising since all people sin and fall short of the glory of God (Romans 3:23).

If you have a hard time knowing if a sentence is true, picture Jesus standing in front of you. Would He say, "You're right, you *are* a failure, the worst failure I've ever seen in my life"? No, He wouldn't.

He'd say, "My beloved, I'm so glad you came to me for help. Why don't we work together on this sin problem of yours?"

Let me show you how I would truth journal the example we just looked at. To make it easier to follow, I'll record the truth after each sentence. Here goes:

Truth Journaling

1. I can't believe I did that.
Truth: I don't know why I can't believe it since I've been practicing this habit for the last 10 YEARS!!!!! Unless God performs a miracle and breaks this habit in an instant, I'll have to accept the fact that I will mess up at times.

2. I'm such a failure.
Truth: No, I'm not. I'm a delightful child of God. His beloved. His bride. His workmanship. I am not defined by what I do, but by who I am in Christ. And in Him, I'm deeply loved, even when I fail.

3. I'll never be able to break this habit.
Truth: This is not true!! I can do all things through Him who strengthens me! The God who was powerful enough to create a whole universe, is definitely powerful enough to help me break this habit. I just need to keep going back to Him again and again for help, and He will change me in *His* time. He who began a good work in me *will* complete it (Philippians 1:6).

4. I try and try and nothing happens.
Truth: That's not true. I just went a week without breaking my boundaries. That's amazing. Although I'm not changing as quickly as I'd like to

change, I *am* changing. God will continue to strengthen me, and one day I will be living in victory with this habit. Believe that!

5. *This time is just like all the other times.*

Truth: No it's not. Because this time I'm fighting with spiritual weapons. I'm bringing my thoughts captive to the truth, and the truth will set me free!!

6. *Why do I even bother?*

Truth: Because God wants me to bother. He wants a holy Barb so I can love Him and others better. But He also wants me to develop the habit of going to Him for help with life. So this isn't just about victory with the habit. It's also about growing closer to God and learning to rely on Him. Every failure is an opportunity for that to happen.

7. *I should just give up.*

Truth: No. I should keep pressing on because the God who loves me will give me victory! And when that day comes, I will rejoice. Keep pressing on, Barb!

Do you see how truth journaling would encourage me to keep pressing on? Truth journaling takes time, but it's time well spent, because not only is it life changing in terms of our habits and emotions, it's also life changing in terms of our walk with God. It will help you grow closer to Him. If you'd like more help with truth journaling, I have lots of examples of it in *Freedom from Emotional Eating*. Here are a few more tips to help you develop the habit:

Truth Journaling Tips

1. *Don't be a perfectionist.*

This is about truth, not writing style, and you're the only one who will see what you wrote. So just blurt everything out and don't worry about how it looks.

2. Try to keep your initial thoughts brief.

Until you get more experienced, try to keep your initial thoughts to a maximum of ten sentences or so. That way you'll have time to record the truth for each sentence. It's essential to write the truth for each sentence because if you don't, you'll be "lie journaling," not truth journaling.

3. Don't get discouraged when you have to journal the same things over and over again.

As you journal, you'll notice that the same thoughts keep coming up day after day. Don't be surprised by this. Truth journaling is not a "journal once and then you're cured" sort of experience. It can take a lot of truth journaling to take off all those lies that have built up through the years.

4. Don't ignore practical truth.

As you apply the truth to each lie, don't feel like the truth always has to be in a Bible verse form. Sometimes you'll write the truth in the form of a Bible verse, sometimes in the form of a biblical principle, and sometimes it will just be a practical truth. The first truth I wrote in my earlier truth journaling example was a practical truth.

5. Look to the Bible for guidance.

If you get stumped about what to write for the truth, ask yourself, "What would Jesus say?" But be sure to take your ideas for what Jesus would say from the Bible and not the culture or the current thinking of the church.

6. Throw the paper away if it will hurt someone.

As you write, you'll notice a lot of ugly thoughts coming across the pages of your journal. If you think someone might see your truth journal entry and be hurt by it, write it on a piece of paper that can be thrown in the garbage when you're through.

7. Enjoy this as a time of fellowship with God.

Truth journaling can be an incredible time of fellowship with the One who loves you and wants to help. In my own life, truth journaling was what brought me back into intimate fellowship with God after years of not being close to Him.

8. Be patient with the learning process.

Truth journaling takes time to learn, but once you get the hang of it, I think you'll really enjoy it. If you're having a hard time with the process, you may want to consider a different type of truth journaling. I call it the "list method."

With this method, rather than spilling out your thoughts without thinking, you ask yourself one of these questions: What am I thinking that's making me want to do my habit? Or what am I thinking that's making me so angry, discouraged, stressed out, etc.? Or what am I thinking that's making me not want to work on my goal or new habit? Am I believing any lies?

Record the lies and then write down the truth for each lie. I have a blog post on my blog called "Truth Journaling: The List Method" if you'd like to see an example of this type of journaling.

Some people have told me that truth journaling works better for them than the questions, especially when they're tackling a new project and don't really know what lies they're believing. I think it also works better if you're in a real emotional turmoil. Truth journaling isn't as easy to learn as the questions, but it's very rewarding once you learn it. I hope you'll give it a try.

CHAPTER 8

Choosing a Renewing of the Mind Project

S O NOW YOU have some renewing of the mind tools and some ideas for projects. What next? It's time to choose a project. Begin by looking back at the questions you answered in chapter two. Then choose the project you think you'd most like to work on, and answer the following questions with that project in mind.

1. How long have you been struggling with (or working on) this emotion, habit, or goal?

2. How does this habit or emotion negatively affect your life? (If you're working on starting a habit, how does the *lack* of this habit negatively affect your life?)

3. How would gaining victory over this habit, emotion, or goal affect the following?

   a. Your relationship with God

   b. Your relationship with others

   c. Your personal wellbeing and/or health

   d. Your ministry and/or testimony

   e. Your work and/or productivity

Would you like to commit to this project? If not, do this worksheet again for one of your other potential projects. If so, state your goal as clearly as possible below. Here are some examples: 1) I want to stop worrying about my kids. 2) I want to stop being insecure and instead see myself through God's eyes. 3) I want to break free from my porn habit. 4) I want to stop procrastinating.

My goal:

You may have noticed that I didn't ask you to put a completion time for your goal. That's because a renewing of the mind project is different than a regular project. Since God is in charge of transformation, we can't say, "I'm going to stop worrying by October 15th." Instead, we need to keep renewing our mind and wait for God to change us in *His* time.

Sometimes God answers pretty quickly and transformation doesn't take long. Other times, it seems to take forever. So as you work on your project, try to be patient. Often we don't see growth because we're not very diligent about renewing our minds. We can change that.

But other times, transformation comes slowly because God has so many lessons He wants to teach us along the way that it's to His advantage *and* ours to take the long slow route. So as you work on your project, remember that your job is to just do what God asks you to do: Abide in Him. Abide in the Word. Renew your mind. Hide God's Word in your heart. Fight with spiritual weapons. Carry your thoughts captive to the truth. And walk by the Spirit.

God's the one in charge of transformation! In a way that's comforting because it takes the pressure off of us to perform. Our burden is light.

The Next Step

I hope you're getting excited about your project. Not just because it will be wonderful to experience transformation, but also because it will be an incredible time of fellowship with God. Are you ready to begin? Let's go ahead and make a plan. Here's what to do next:

- If you're doing an **emotions project** (anger/annoyance, worry, insecurity, discontentment, etc.), read chapter 9 and fill out the plan in that chapter.

- If you're doing a **breaking a habit project** (emails, Facebook, pornography, texting, computer games, weight loss, etc.), read chapter 10 and fill out the plan in that chapter. (Note: overcoming procrastination is a starting a habit project as you're starting the habit of following your to-do list.)

- If you're doing a **starting a habit or accomplishing a goal project** (writing a book, starting a quiet time habit, etc.), read chapter 11 and fill out the plan in that chapter.

- If you're not sure what category your project fits into, keep reading. I'll be talking about complicated projects in a minute.

When you're through reading your chapter and making your plan, go ahead and read chapter 9 if you haven't already read it, since no mater what project you take on, you'll still have to deal with your emotions. Then read chapter 12 and get started on your project!

Complicated Projects

Sometimes it's hard to determine what category your project fits into. Here's an example: Suppose your goal is to become a more positive person. To explore your goal further, ask yourself, "In what areas of my life am I negative?"

Perhaps you're often annoyed with people. Or maybe you assume you're going to fail at everything you do. Or maybe you're discontent. You could either a) make a commitment to renew your mind every time you're negative or b) focus on just one area of negativity (annoyance, for example). Either way, it would be an emotions project.

Here's another example. Suppose your goal is to step out of your comfort zone. This sounds like a starting a habit goal, and it could be, depending on how you set it up. If you want to make it a starting a habit project, record what you plan to do each week to step out of your comfort zone. For example, you might say, "I'll initiate and be actively involved in one deep conversation a day." You would then renew your mind before you had that conversation and perhaps afterwards as well.

Another way you could approach a comfort zone project would be to ask yourself, "What emotion do I most often feel in uncomfortable situations?" If it's insecurity, you could make it an insecurity project and just renew your mind whenever you feel insecure.

Those are just a couple of examples, but I hope they'll help you analyze your own project. If you can't figure out what category your project falls into, email me at my blog. If I get a lot of emails, I'll try to do a podcast on that subject.

A Renewing of the Mind Habit Project

If the thought of doing any kind of project is scary and you're having a hard time making yourself fill out the worksheets in this book, consider doing a starting a habit project to develop a renewing of the mind habit.

Make a goal of renewing your mind once or twice a day about anything that comes up during the day. If you don't feel like following through on your commitment, use the starting a habit questions and Bible verses to renew your mind *about* the renewing of the mind.

If you decide to do this, read Chapter 11 and fill out the plan in that chapter. If you'd like specific Bible verses for a renewing of the mind or quiet time habit, look at the Bible verses that go with the lack of importance questions.

CHAPTER 9

An Emotions Project

ONE OF THE things that most surprised me about the renewing of the mind was how God used the truth to actually *change* me. Not just my actions, but also my emotions.

I started with a renewing of the mind project for anger. As I took off the lies I believed about life and people and learned to see both from God's perspective, I found myself enjoying people more and more. I was no longer annoyed all the time, and when I was, it was a minor feeling, not a major this-is-completely-ruining-my-day sort of response.

The other thing that happened was that for the first time in my life I learned what it was like to live in peace. I loved that peace so much that whenever I became annoyed my first impulse was to go to God for help. And while it was hard to let go of my annoyance in the beginning, it became much easier later on.

An emotions project is rewarding to work on because you often see growth quickly. For that reason, it's often easier to work on than a habits project. Here's the basic process if you want to work on your negative emotions:

1. Set a renewing of the mind goal.

There are three different ways to set a renewing of the mind goal for an emotion. You can renew your mind a) whenever you experience the emotion, b) whenever you experience the emotion in a particular situation, or c) a certain number of times a day.

Here's an example: Suppose your goal is to stop worrying. If you're a lightweight worrier, make a goal to renew your mind every time you worry. If you're a heavyweight worrier, consider focusing on just one area of worry: I'll renew my mind every time I worry about finances, for example. Or I'll renew my mind every time I worry about the future of our country.

Your goal should be big enough that you're renewing your mind at least once a day, but not so big that you have to renew your mind twenty times a day! You could also set a number goal: I'll renew my mind two times a day, for example.

2. Renew your mind.

The second step is to renew your mind every time you said you would. If you can't renew your mind right away, do it as soon as possible after you experience the emotion. It's much easier to let go of negative emotions if we catch them early. Once we hit the majorly upset stage, it's hard to even think. And we need to think in order to renew our minds.

As you renew your mind, remember that this isn't a "check renew your mind off the list" experience. Your goal is to see life from a biblical perspective, and especially in the beginning of your project, this can take a bit of time.

When I first started renewing my mind for anger, I would often be up in the middle of the night talking to God, trying to see life from His perspective. It wasn't uncommon to spend an hour renewing my mind before I finally came to peace and was able to let go of my anger.

But after a month or two, it was pretty easy. I could usually let go of it in five or ten minutes. So this is one of those things that gets easier with practice.

We've already talked about different ways to renew your mind, but how would this look in practice? Let's say you've made a commitment to renew your mind every time you're insecure. You're feeling insecure right now, so at the first possible opportunity you'll renew your mind.

You might truth journal. You might pray through some of the insecurity Bible verses. You might go through some of the insecurity questions. Or you might do something else that helps you look at life from a biblical perspective.

Hopefully, at the end of your time with God, you'll be seeing yourself as He sees you—because when you see yourself as He sees you, you'll no longer feel insecure.

Don't get flustered if you can't come to that point right away. It takes time to take off those lies you've believed all your life. Just keep plugging away and eventually you'll start seeing life—and yourself—from His perspective.

If you'd like to keep track of your renewing of the mind progress, I've included charts for that purpose at the back of this book.

3. Accept what you need to accept.

This step came as a shock to me when I first started renewing my mind. I was under the mistaken impression that if I just worked hard enough, I could solve all my problems. But this isn't true. God hasn't given us the power to fix everything we want to fix.

Sometimes our only choice is to accept what's happening with a hopeful attitude or a despairing attitude because, like it or not, it's happening. It's far easier to accept hard things with a hopeful attitude if life is about God.

In the questions and Bible verses portion of this book, I've included "possible things you'll need to accept" for each emotion. This section will give you ideas of what you may need to accept to break free from that emotion.

Often what we need to accept will seem *un*acceptable. Everything within us will cry out, "What?? That's ridiculous! I shouldn't have to put up with that!"

We think that because we've grown up in a world that tells us every day that we deserve the good life, that we shouldn't have to suffer, and that we shouldn't have to put up with anything from anybody.

This is directly contrary to Scripture, which says things like, "Lay down your lives out of love for the brethren," and "Be content in any situation," and "Take up your cross and follow me." The interesting thing about the Bible, though, is that it works.

When we demand our "rights" and refuse to accept anything less, we're constantly unhappy. Life never lives up to our unrealistic expectations for it. We're always left wanting more.

But when we give up our rights, willing to live any sort of life for God, we're content. We bask in the fruit of the Spirit, and we don't need a certain lifestyle to make us happy.

On both a practical level and a spiritual level, life is better when we give up our demands and accept—and even embrace—a less-than-ideal life when necessary. But how do you get to that point? The next step will help.

4. Pray with thanksgiving.

If I were to pick one passage that has helped me the most with my negative emotions, it would be Philippians 4:6-7:

> *Be anxious for nothing, but in everything by prayer and supplication with thanksgiving let your requests be made known to God. And the peace of God, which surpasses all comprehension, will guard your hearts and your minds in Christ Jesus.*

I first learned about the power of this passage when I was writing the worry chapter in *Freedom from Emotional Eating*. I tried praying with thanksgiving for some of my own worries, and it helped me more than anything I'd ever done to let go of my worries.

As I made my requests to God and quickly moved into thanksgiving, I found my worries slipping away. Praying with thanksgiving helped me remember that life was about God, that He was in control, and that I could trust Him no matter what happened.

As you pray with thanksgiving, thank God for your current blessings, but also thank Him for who He is in the midst of your troublesome situation and how His character blesses you.

It also helps to think of all the ways He's helped you in the past. If you can't think of things to be thankful for, check out my blog post entitled "20 Things to be Thankful For When Life is Hard."

5. Do what you can on a practical level to make life better.

One of the things we can thank God for is that we often *can* do something to improve our day-to-day life. If you're in a difficult situation, ask yourself, "Is there anything I can do on a practical level to make life better?"

Here are a few examples: If you're stressed, could you get rid of some activities? If you're annoyed, could you add some boundaries to that relationship? If you're worried about finances, could you go to a financial planning class?

If you're fearful, could you go to someone for help? If you're insecure, could you stop reading or viewing things that make you feel insecure? Or could you work on changing something, as long as God approves of the change?

Think about living the best life possible within the context of making life all about loving God and doing His will. In other words, don't try to create a *life* that will make you happy.

Go to God to get your needs met. Then, within the safety of His arms, reach out and see what you can do to improve your situation.

Speaking of going to God to get your needs met, are you ready to make your plan for going to God for help with your emotions? If you are, go ahead and fill out the plan below.

My Plan

1. What is your goal? (You've already recorded this in Chapter 8.)

2. How often would you like to renew your mind? (See step one in this chapter.) Circle one of the following:

    a. Every time I experience this emotion

    b. Every time I experience the emotion in this situation: _____
    _____

    c. _____ times a day

3. What time of day would be best for you to renew your mind?

4. As you work on this emotion, what are some things you might need to accept with a hopeful, life-is-about-God attitude? (If you need ideas, turn to your emotion in the questions and Bible verses section of the book and look at "possible things you'll need to accept.")

5. What Bible verses could you memorize to help you with your goal? List two or three verses.

6. Can you think of any practical things you can do to make life better, within the context of making life all about God and doing His will? (See step five for ideas.)

7. When would you like to start working on your project?

CHAPTER 10

A Stopping a Habit Project

I'M AT OUR local coffee shop this morning, trying to write this chapter. I just spent the last hour writing, with nothing to show for it I just can't figure out how to write this chapter.

After taking a break to renew my mind with the disappointment questions in this book, I realized, *Writing a book is a lot like breaking a habit.*

I can't make myself write a good book no matter how hard I try because I'm not a naturally gifted writer. Nor am I naturally disciplined.

But I *can* keep putting in my time each day: planning, thinking, praying, putting words on paper, and renewing my mind whenever I can't make myself write.

And you know what? That's all God asks. He's the one in charge of how the book turns out, not me. I just have to put the words on the paper. My burden is light.

It's the same with breaking habits. You can't break your habit. You're not good in this area of your life. You're not naturally disciplined. But you know what? You don't have to be.

All you have to do is put in your time each day: try to follow your boundaries, renew your mind when you can't, repent and ask forgiveness if you sin, and keep abiding in God.

That's all He asks of you. God's the one in charge of how quickly you change. And that makes your burden light.

So as you think about breaking your habit, before you even read the steps below, please, please, please, *give yourself grace.* God loves you as you are. He delights in you. He is shouting over you with joy *right now.* Even though you're still entrenched in that habit!

And God, the King of the Universe, the Creator of everything you see, *that* God is fully capable of helping you break your habit. So don't worry. Just keep doing what He asks you to do and wait for Him to transform you. Let's take a look at the basic process of breaking a habit:

1. Set boundaries

According to thefreedictionary.com, a boundary is "something that indicates a border or a limit." A playground fence is an example of a boundary. It limits where the kids can play. But that's not all it does. It also cramps their style.

Those little kids would love to run out in the street and look at all those fun, noisy cars—but the fence holds them in and says, "No, kids, you can't play in the street."

That doesn't mean the fence is bad. On the contrary, the fence makes their lives *better* because it protects them from harm. The same is true for us. Boundaries in the areas of our habits make our lives better because they keep us safe.

Yes, they cramp our style, but you know what? Our style needs to be cramped. Because there are consequences to doing "what we want when we want" with our habits. Just think of your own habit. What happens when you do it as much as you want to do it?

Do you live a wonderful, peace-filled life, thanking God every day for your habit? Or do you live a stressful, regretful life, full of the consequences of too much habit?

I think we can all relate to that second question because we've all been in that sinking boat—and it's not a fun place to be.

That's why the first thing you need to do if you want to gain victory over your habit is to establish boundaries. The boundaries should tell you **how often** you can do your habit and **how much** of your habit you can do.

If your habit's a sin, the boundaries are obvious: no habit period. If your habit isn't a sin, it's a little more complicated. Here are some questions to help you come up with boundaries for your habit:

1. How much time do you think God wants you to spend on this habit?

2. What would be the best amount if you had the control to actually follow through with it?

3. What's the best amount for maximum benefit with minimum consequences?

Talk to God about it and see if you can come up with a good concrete set of boundaries. Here are some examples of boundaries:

- **Emails:** I can check my emails 3 times a day but I have to answer them every time I check them.

- **Facebook:** I can be on Facebook for 20 minutes a day.

- **Texts:** I can look at texts in social settings only if I'm expecting an urgent text.

- **Computer games:** I can spend 2 hours a week playing computer games.

- **Work:** I can't work after 5:00.

It's important to set boundaries if you want to break free from (or limit) your habit, but unless you have iron willpower, you'll need the next step.

2. Renew your mind again and again and again.

Although boundaries are helpful and necessary, they aren't enough. Why? Because we can't make ourselves follow them! If we want to be transformed, we'll need to renew our minds so that we'll actually *want* to follow them.

There are three ways you can approach the renewing of the mind for your habit: You can renew your mind a) whenever you're tempted to break your boundaries, b) whenever you actually break them, or c) a certain number of times a day.

If possible, try to renew your mind in a journal. Something about the act of writing things down helps to drill the truth into our heads. You could truth journal, write out Scripture prayers, write down some of the Bible verses and record how they apply to your habit, or go through some of the questions in this book.

If it's too hard to figure out what set of Bible verses or questions to use, just start at the beginning and do two or three sets a day. Maybe one in the morning to get the day started with the right attitude, then one at lunch for reinforcement, and another after dinner.

The more you fill your mind with truth, the less tempted you'll be to do your habit. If you'd like more ideas of different ways to renew your mind, check out the renewing of the mind tools tab at my blog. If you'd like to keep track of your renewing of the mind progress, I've included charts for that purpose at the back of this book.

3. Go to God for help with life.

One of the reasons it's so hard to break free from our habits is that we have a tendency to go to them for help with life. Just think of your own habit. How often do you do it when you're stressed? Or when you're feeling insecure or depressed? Or when you're procrastinating?

With an overeating habit, we call this behavior *emotional eating*. In the breaking a habit questions, I call it *emotional habiting*. If you struggle with emotional habiting, ask yourself, "What emotion am I feeling right now?" Then use that set of questions and Bible verses to renew your mind.

If you can't figure out what emotion you're experiencing, think back over the events of the day. What did you do? Who did you talk to you? What did you read? Try to pinpoint the moment you started feeling distressed and that will help you determine which set of questions and Bible verses would work best.

4. Look for practical ways to minimize temptation.

Think of the habit you're trying to break. Is there anything you can do on a practical level to help you follow your boundaries?

Here are some examples: If you're trying to break an Internet habit, you could unplug the router and place it in a hard-to-get-to location whenever you're tempted to break your boundaries.

If you're trying to break a making out habit, you could make sure you're never alone with your boyfriend or girlfriend unless you're out in public.

If you're trying to break a Facebook habit, you could download an app such as Anti-Social, which will turn off problem sites for a specific period of time.

These are just a few ideas. Can you think of any practical ways to minimize temptation for your own habit? If you're doing this book as a group study, brainstorm ideas with your group. If you're doing the project by yourself, look for ideas on the Internet.

5. Get an accountability partner.

If you can't make yourself renew your mind, consider getting an accountability partner: someone who will ask you every day, "Did you renew your mind?" If you think it would be helpful, ask them to hold you accountable to following your boundaries, too. You might also want to consider forming a small accountability group to work on a project together.

6. Remember that growth isn't a straight line.

Picture a stock market chart. It never goes straight up, even if the stock is soaring. It's the same way with growth. We have a bunch of good days, then a bad day, and maybe even a string of bad days. But as long as we keep going back to God and renewing our minds, the overall trend will be up.

As you work on breaking your habit, think of this as a war rather than a skirmish. In any long drawn-out war, there are victories and defeats, and it doesn't always look like you're going to win the war.

Don't get discouraged when it looks like you're losing the battle. God is faithful. He will help you break this habit! Just keep going to Him for help every time you need it.

7. Don't beat yourself up when you break your boundaries.

This is probably the most important tip in this whole chapter: Renew your mind *every single time* you break your boundaries. The sooner the better. Here's what happens when we don't renew our minds: We either beat ourselves up, or we throw caution to the wind and start breaking our boundaries right and left.

Something about that one little failure triggers a whole series of failures. *I've already broken my boundaries once*, we think, *so I might as well do it again.* That's why it's so important to renew our minds right away. So we not only see our habit from God's perspective, but also our failure.

This is especially important with habits we consider "really bad." Because with those habits, we tend to go into "I can't believe I did this terrible thing, no one else is this bad, I'm such a horrible Christian" mode. This is not productive, nor is it truthful!

The truth is, we're *all* sinners. And one sin isn't worse than another. The church may have a continuum of sins with some worse than others, but God doesn't. In His eyes, sin is sin. So don't feel like your sin is the bottom of the barrel. We're all at the bottom of the barrel!

If you have a tendency to beat yourself up, remember that Satan is the condemner of the saints, not God. God is the lover and forgiver and grace-giver of the saints (Revelations 12:10, Romans 8:1, John 8:1-11, Ephesians 2:8-9, John 3:16-17). As you work on your breaking-a-habit project, don't forget to embrace His grace. You'll need it!

8. Persevere.

Every once in awhile, God will perform a miracle and give us instant victory over our habits. But this is rare. Most of the time He allows us to walk the heavily traveled "this is a growing experience" path.

Don't despair if that's the path you're on. Remember, God works all things together for good (Romans 8:28), He loves you, and He's walking that path right alongside you.

As you work together, you'll grow closer to Him and more dependent on Him. That's a beautiful thing, and a lesson you might not learn if He were to change you with the blink of His eye.

So be steadfast. Keep going back to Him for help. And trust Him to change you in His time. Are you ready to get started on your breaking-a-habit project? Let's begin by making a plan.

My Plan

1. What is your goal?

2. What are your boundaries? (See step one in this chapter.)

3. How often would you like to renew your mind? (See step two.) Circle one of the following:

    a. Every time I feel like breaking my boundaries.

    b. Every time I break my boundaries.

    c. _____ times a day.

4. Would you like an accountability partner? If so, whom could you ask?

5. What Bible verses could you memorize to help with your goal? List two or three verses.

6. Is there anything you can do on a practical level to minimize temptation? (See step four.)

7. Can you think of any other books you could read or Bible studies you could do to help you with this project? (Note: See pages 213-214 for additional resources.)

8. What will you do if you break your boundaries? (I'm hoping you'll say, "Renew my mind," and not, "Beat myself up, think about what a loser I am, and give up!!")

9. What can you hope in as you begin this project? (Philippians 1:6)

10. When will you start this project?

CHAPTER 11

A Starting a Habit
or Accomplishing
a Goal Project

OME PEOPLE SEEM to have a knack for making goals and crossing them off their lists. I don't! The only way I can accomplish anything is to keep going back to God again and again for strength, truth, and moral support. I wrote the starting a habit questions in this book to help me with that.

If you look at the questions, you'll notice that I don't have tips like I do for breaking a habit. That's because I don't know enough yet to give you any tips! I'm just barely hanging on myself, still struggling to follow my to-do list and renewing my mind every day to make that possible.

But I can say that the questions work. You can use them to go to God for help with accomplishing goals, developing new habits, and overcoming procrastination by learning to follow your to-do list. The process is the same for all them. Here it is:

1. Research your goal or habit.

Depending on the habit or goal you're working on, it may be helpful to do some research before you get started. Research will accomplish two purposes: First, it will give you some good how-to help. And second, it will motivate you.

If you're working on a prayer habit, for example, you could read how-to books on prayer or biographies of great people of prayer such as George Mueller or Brother Lawrence (*Practicing the Presence of God*).

If you want to write a book, you could read how-to books about writing. The authors will give you time-saving advice and inspire you as you catch their excitement for the process.

2. Make a plan (or to-do list).

After you've spent some time researching your habit or goal, you'll be better prepared to develop a plan. If you're working on a habit, your plan will be pretty simple: Have a 30-minute quiet time each morning, for example. Or exercise once a day before 11:00 am.

If you're working on overcoming procrastination, make a list each morning and renew your mind every time you don't feel like following it. Try to keep your list short at first (3-5 items) so you'll have a better chance of finishing it.

If you're working on a goal, your plan will be a little more complicated. Think of all the steps necessary to complete your project, and then write those steps down. Here's an example of a plan you could make to accomplish the goal of organizing your clothing closet:

1. Take all the clothes out.

2. For each clothing item, ask the following questions: a) Do I need this? b) Do I wear this? c) Do I love this?

3. Get rid of any clothes I don't need, wear, or love.

4. Hang the rest back up in the closet.

5. Make a commitment to not buy anything new unless I get rid of something first.

6. Enjoy my nice decluttered closet!

Do you see how breaking the project into steps would automatically make it easier to accomplish?

After you make a list of steps, try to wipe the list from your memory and just focus on the next step. If you can't get yourself to do the next step, renew your mind.

3. Renew your mind every time you don't feel like following the plan.

One of the easiest ways to renew your mind is to go to the Table of Contents, look through all the lies I've listed under the starting a habit questions, choose one that applies to your reason for not wanting to work on your goal, habit, or to-do list, and then renew your mind with those questions.

The emotions questions and Bible verses may also be helpful, especially stress, frustration, feeling inadequate, and self-condemnation. If you'd like to keep track of your renewing of the mind progress, I've included charts for that purpose at the back of this book.

Although you can use the questions to make yourself do things like decluttering closets, those types of goals probably won't do anything for your relationship with God or others (unless your spouse is annoyed by your messy closet).

If one of your main goals for a project is to draw closer to God, an emotions or breaking a habit project might be a better option.

4. Work hard, and keep your eyes on the finish line.

One of the lies we often believe is "Life should be easy." This is a problem when we start working on a new habit or goal because we have unrealistic expectations for that goal. We think that all we need to do is set our goals and then—boom—we'll accomplish them.

Nothing could be further from the truth. In reality, success is more like a stock market chart. First, it's not guaranteed.

And second, even if we do succeed, it's not a straight up line. At times it looks like we'll never succeed. And at other times it looks like we're going to succeed like crazy, only to have our hopes dashed the following week.

The best way to stay sane is to keep our eyes on the *real* finish line—eternity with God (Hebrews 12:1-2). The more we keep our eyes on Him and walk in fellowship with Him, the more we'll enjoy the process.

The more we keep our eyes on our goals, feeling like we *have* to succeed, the less we'll enjoy the process. I've been struggling with this myself for the last few years. How do I keep God first while pursuing my goal of writing books?

I don't know how many hours I've spent renewing my mind on things related to writing—probably in the hundreds category. But I've had to do that to stay close to God because of all of the temptations to make life about things other than God that have come into my life because of writing.

If you're working on a habit that will bring you closer to God—having a quiet time, prayer, or a renewing of the mind habit, for example—you won't have to worry.

But if you're working on a habit or goal that has the potential to draw you away from God, you'll have to be careful. Work hard, but remember that life is about loving God and others.

If you find yourself getting obsessed with your goal, set boundaries on how often you can work on it and renew your mind whenever you feel obsessed. The reward/obsession, workaholism, and greed/lust questions and Bible verses are all helpful for that purpose. If you're ready to get started on your habit or goal, begin by making a plan.

My Plan

1. What is your goal?

2. Can you think of any topics you could research on the Internet to help you with this habit or goal? Can you think of any books you could read?

3. What is your plan? In other words, what days of the week will you work on this goal or habit? What time of day will you work on it, and how long will you spend working on it?

4. How often would you like to renew your mind? (See step three in this chapter.) Circle one of the following:

   a. Every time I don't feel like working on my plan.

   b. _____ times a day.

5. If you're working on a goal, what steps do you need to take to accomplish your goal? (See step two.)

6. If you can't make yourself work on your habit, goal, or to-do list, what will you do? (I'm hoping you'll say, "Renew your mind," and not, "Give up and go out for donuts!")

7. When will you start this project?

CHAPTER 12

What Else Does the Bible Say About Transformation?

B Y NOW, MANY of you have made your plans, and you're working on your project. I hope it's going well. But I've done enough of my own projects to know that it may *not* be going well! The truth is, a renewing of the mind project is a lot different than a skill based project, such as putting in a garden or making a scrapbook.

With a renewing of the mind project, you're working on changing something you may have been doing all your life. That's a lot harder to accomplish than a normal project. In order to reach your goal, you'll need all the help you can get. Let's go back to that list we talked about in chapter 3, and see what else the Bible tells us to do if we want to be transformed.

We've talked about several of the items on that list already: renewing our minds, memorizing Scripture, and taking our thoughts captive to the truth. In this chapter, we'll take a look at the rest of the list:

1. Fighting with spiritual weapons (Ephesians 6:10-18)

2. Abiding in God's Word (John 8:31-32)

3. Abiding in God (John 15:1-5)

4. Walking by the Spirit (Galatians 5:16-25)

We'll begin with spiritual weapons. To get a context for this, let's look at Ephesians 6:10-18:

> *Finally, be strong in the Lord and in the strength of His might. Put on the full armor of God, so that you will be able to stand firm against the schemes of the devil. For our struggle is not against flesh and blood, but against the rulers, against the powers, against the world forces of this darkness, against the spiritual forces of wickedness in the heavenly places. Therefore, take up the full armor of God, so that you will be able to resist in the evil day, and having done everything, to stand firm. Stand firm therefore, having girded your loins with truth, and having put on the breastplate of righteousness, and having shod your feet with the preparation of the gospel of peace; in addition to all, taking up the shield of faith with which you will be able to extinguish all the flaming arrows of the evil one. And take the helmet of salvation, and the sword of the Spirit, which is the word of God. With all prayer and petition pray at all times in the Spirit, and with this in view, be on the alert with all perseverance and petition for all the saints. (Ephesians 6:10-18)*

You've heard the phrase, "Don't try to do it in your own strength." Paul agrees. He begins by telling us to be strong in the Lord and in the strength of *His* might. Why? Because we have an enemy. An enemy so powerful that our own meager strength won't be enough to defeat it.

In a way this is comforting. Just think of that habit you've been trying to break forever. Do you ever beat yourself up for breaking your boundaries? The truth is, it's not surprising when you break your boundaries, because you have all those spiritual forces working against you (Ephesians 6:12).

Or what about that negative emotion that paralyzes you? Do you ever beat yourself up because "a Christian shouldn't be struggling with that emotion"? The truth is, it's not surprising that you're struggling with that emotion, because you have all those spiritual forces working against you.

Satan loves to see us struggle because that opens up a whole new door for him to attack. He's the accuser of the brethren (Revelations 12:10), and he uses our weaknesses to help us down the path of hopelessness, despair, and self-condemnation.

When we beat ourselves up, we're playing right into his hands. Our best hope is to stop beating ourselves up, go to God for help, and engage in warfare. Fight with the weapons God has provided. Let's take a look at those weapons.

Fight With Spiritual Weapons

1. Gird your loins with truth.

First Paul tells us to gird our loins with truth. This is something men did back in the New Testament days to prepare for battle. They would reach down, grab the bottom of their robe, pull it up between their legs, and secure it at their waist with a belt. This would free them up to fight without their robes getting in the way.

The timing was important. Can you imagine a soldier in the heat of the battle saying, "Just a minute, guys, I need to get my robe out of the way"? He'd be dead meat in no time. No, if he wanted to be successful, he had to gird his loins *before* going into battle.

So how does this apply to our projects? Simple. We need to do the same thing if we want to be successful in fighting the enemy: We need to prepare with truth before the battle ever begins.

Here's how this works on a practical level: If you're working on a habit and anticipating a tempting situation, renew your mind right before you enter into that situation. If you're working on an emotion and have a difficult day ahead of you, renew your mind early in the day before you've even experienced that emotion. If you've already broken your boundaries, prepare for the temptation of beating yourself up by renewing your mind as soon as possible after you break your boundaries.

If you'd like some other ideas of how to prepare with truth, I have two posts on this subject under the Renewing of the Mind Tools tab at my blog (Preparation Truth: Part 1 and 2).

2. Put on the breastplate of righteousness.

You've heard the phrase, "bad company corrupts good morals" (1 Corinthians 15:33). The idea is that if you hang around with people who are sinning, you'll start sinning yourself. Living a life without boundaries is like hanging around with bad company. It's a way of opening ourselves up to temptation.

Just think of your own habit. What happens when you drop your boundaries and say, "I'm going to do *what* I want *when* I want?" You get hurt, right? Those boundaries were a protection. They protected your heart from sin.

Boundaries are like a fence. When you let them down, it provides an opening for the enemy to get into your life and cause damage. Righteousness—or holy behavior—protects us from the enemy. And boundaries help us keep our behavior in holy territory.

3. Shod your feet with the preparation of the gospel of peace

When I first got serious about breaking my overeating habit, I was already having daily quiet times. But every once in awhile I would miss one. What surprised me was how vital those morning quiet times were to the success of following my boundaries. Almost without fail, the days I missed my morning quiet times were the days I also broke my boundaries.

When we prepare our minds with the gospel at the beginning of the day, we're in a much better spot to stand against spiritual attack. It's not a guarantee that we'll stand, but it definitely helps.

Jesus is our example. He was constantly leaving the crowds to spend time with His Father, and He was full of the Spirit when he went into the desert to be tempted by Satan (Luke 4:1). He had prepared with the gospel of peace, and He was ready for the attack that was to come.

4. Take up the shield of faith.

This is one of the most important defensive weapons, and one we often forget to use. If you work on a project, you'll desperately need the shield of faith because the enemy will send you arrows on a regular basis that say, "You can't do this! Look at you! You just failed! Who are you kidding? You'll never change!! You're such a sorry excuse for a Christian!"

When those times come—and they will—take up your shield of faith and believe that God loves you and accepts you even in the midst of your sin (John 8:1-11, Romans 5:8, Romans 8:1) and that He who began a good work in you will complete it (Philippians 1:6). The hopelessness, self-condemnation, and failure questions and Bible verses will all help when you're feeling like you'll never change.

5. Take the helmet of salvation.

Everything I wrote in this book presupposes that you're already a Christian. If you've repented of your sin, confessed Jesus as Lord, and surrendered your life to God, you're in a powerful position. Jesus died to set you free from the power of sin, and He accomplished His purpose. But you need to be in that "saved" position to have access to His power. If you're not in that position, this is a good time to make that change! If you'd like help with that, visit a local pastor or contact me through the about tab at my blog.

6. Take up the sword of the Spirit, which is the word of God.

Truth is so powerful that Paul mentions it as both a defensive weapon (gird your loins with truth) and an offensive weapon (take up the sword of the Spirit). We saw Jesus using the word of God as an offensive weapon in the midst of his own spiritual battle (Matthew 4:1-11). We can do the same. We talked about how to do that in Chapter 5.

7. Pray at all times in the Spirit.

Prayer is powerful. Paul tells us to pray at all times, not just for ourselves but also for each other. If you have an accountability partner or a group that you're doing your project with, one of the most powerful things you can do is to pray for each other. Share your struggles and your prayer needs and lift each other up in prayer as you work on your projects together.

Abide in God's Word

In John 8:31-32, Jesus tells us to abide in God's word and the truth will set us free. The Greek word for *abide* is the same word used for living in a house. The idea is that we don't just visit the Word for ten minutes a day. Instead, we *live* in it. Meditate on it. Chew on it as we walk through the day.

Let it fill us and change the way we think about life. Let it fill us and change the way we think about our habits. And let it fill us and change the way we think about others and ourselves.

I've included bits of the Word in this book. Bits that you can use in the midst of spiritual battle. But it's also important to be studying the Bible and soaking in it each day.

I find when I'm doing a project that all kinds of passages apply to my project that you wouldn't think would apply. So as I take in the Word in my morning quiet times, I'm constantly thinking, *How does this apply to my current struggle?* I'll often journal about the passages I read and record any insights God gives me, as that helps me to remember what He says.

Walk in the Spirit and Abide in Jesus

We live in an instant society. We're so used to getting what we want quickly and easily that we often expect to reach our goals without a lot of effort on our part. But life doesn't always work that way.

Jesus tells us that we can't bear fruit unless we abide in Him (John 15:4). Paul tells us that if we want to receive the fruit of the Spirit, we need to walk in the Spirit (Galatians 5:16-25). Walking and abiding aren't instant activities. They take time.

Do you remember at the beginning of Chapter 10 when I took the time to go to God for help right away in the coffee shop after being discouraged about writing? Yesterday was a completely different story.

Once again I was discouraged about writing. It was 9:00 in the morning, I was at home, and I had gotten off track with my writing schedule after camping for four days and then having a long to-do list when I got back. I was feeling like I would never finish writing this book and even if I did finish it, that it would be a worthless book, so why bother?

Instead of going to God for help—abiding in Jesus and walking in the

Spirit—I spent the entire day avoiding Him. First I procrastinated for several hours. Then I did a bit of work around the house. Then I procrastinated for a few more hours, wrote for about 30 minutes, and called it a day.

No abiding in Jesus. No walking in the Spirit. No renewing my mind.

Because I chose to rely on my own resources instead of going to God for help, I missed out on the fruit of the Spirit. Here's what I would have gotten if I'd chosen to abide in Jesus and walk in the Spirit: love, joy, peace, patience, kindness, goodness, faithfulness, gentleness, and self-control (Galatians 5:22-23).

Just what I needed.

But since I chose to walk in procrastination and avoidance, this is what I got instead: discouragement, stress, self-condemnation, hopelessness, a lack of self-control, and a wasted day.

Would it have taken time to go to God and abide in Him? Of course! But that would have been time well spent—not just in terms of what I would have accomplished, but also in terms of my relationship with Him. I finally worked through things with God this morning, but life would have been so much better if I had gone to Him the moment I felt like giving up yesterday.

As you work on your project, try to abide in Jesus and walk in the Spirit. You'll be tempted to give up. You'll be tempted to beat yourself up. And you'll be tempted to sink into depression and hopelessness. This is something we all struggle with.

The way to avoid it is to go to God for help as soon as you feel that first emotional glitch. It may be a bit of discouragement, a touch of annoyance, a glimmer of worry, or a hint of failure. As soon as you feel that first inkling of trouble, go to God for help. It's so much easier to work through a little bit of trouble than a lot of trouble.

If you look closely at the fruit of the Spirit, that's what we all need, whether we're working on stopping a habit, starting a habit, accomplishing a goal, or breaking free from an emotion. God doesn't give us a full measure of fruit the minute we commit our lives to Him. Instead, He gives it to us day by day as we walk through life with Him and abide in Him.

My hope and prayer for you is that this project will be a time of walking and abiding in God. That as you develop the habit of going to Him for help with your project, you'll also be developing a closer and more intimate relationship with Him. Shall we go to Him together?

STARTING A
HABIT

OR

PURSUING A
GOAL

QUESTIONS
AND
BIBLE VERSES

Boredom

1. If real life were like a romantic comedy or an action thriller, what % of your life would be exciting?

2. What % of the average person's life is exciting?

3. Think of all the believers in the Bible. What % of their lives was fun and exciting?

4. Do you think you have unrealistic expectations for life? Explain.

5. If your main goal in life were to have fun, what would you do with your time right now?

6. What do you think God wants you to do with your time right now?

7. Why do you think He wants you to do that?

8. Are you willing to be bored for God and others if that's what you need to do to love them well?

9. Is there anything you need to accept about life?

10. What can you thank God for in this situation?

Bible Verses

Mark 10:43b-45 Whoever wishes to become great among you shall be your servant; and whoever wishes to be first among you shall be slave of all. For even the Son of Man did not come to be served, but to serve, and to give His life a ransom for many.

Philippians 1:21 For to me, to live is Christ and to die is gain.

Philippians 4:11-13 Not that I speak from want, for I have learned to be content in whatever circumstances I am. I know how to get along with humble means, and I also know how to live in prosperity; in any and every circumstance I have learned the secret of being filled and going hungry, both of having abundance and suffering need. I can do all things through Him who strengthens me.

Colossians 3:2 Set your mind on the things above, not on the things that are on earth.

1 John 3:16 We know love by this, that He laid down His life for us; and we ought to lay down our lives for the brethren.

See also: indulgence, beginning of day stress, and discontentment.

Decisions

Note: The beginning of the day stress questions may be more helpful for "What should I do today?" decisions.

1. Why are you having a hard time making this decision?

2. What are your options?

3. Do you have enough information to make a good decision? If not, what information do you need to gather?

4. What do others you respect think about your options?

5. Are you tempted to do something just because it's expected of you? If so, do you also think it's a good thing to do? Why or why not?

6. Does the Bible speak at all to your decision?

    a. **Yes:** If so, what does it say? Are you willing to do what the Bible says even if you have to sacrifice to do it?

    b. **No:** If not, does God give you the freedom to make your own decision?

7. Do you think God would prefer one choice over another? If so, why?

8. How will you know if you've made a good decision? (Remember, the idea that you should expect everything in life to go smoothly is a modern concept, not a biblical concept.)

9. Is this one of those situations where you can't really know what's best?

10. What's the worst thing that can happen if you make what appears to be the wrong decision?

11. Can God redeem bad decisions?

12. What will have to sacrifice or accept to make this decision and not keep second-guessing yourself?

13. What can you thank God for in this situation? (Once you make your decision, focus on being thankful for the good things about the option you chose.)

Bible Verses

Proverbs 11:14 Where there is no guidance the people fall, but in abundance of counselors there is victory.

Proverbs 19:21 Many plans are in a man's heart, but the counsel of the Lord will stand.

Proverbs 20:5 A plan in the heart of a man is like deep water, but a man of understanding draws it out.

1 Corinthians 10:31 Whether, then, you eat or drink or whatever you do, do all to the glory of God.

James 1:5 But if any of you lacks wisdom, let him ask of God, who gives to all generously and without reproach, and it will be given to him.

James 4:13-15 Come now, you who say, "Today or tomorrow we will go to such and such a city, and spend a year there and engage in business and make a profit." Yet you do not know what your life will be like tomorrow. You are just a vapor that appears for a little while and then vanishes away. Instead, you ought to say, "If the Lord wills, we will live and also do this or that."

See also: people pleasing, perfectionism, and greed/lust.

Disappointment

Note: Depending on what you're disappointed with, the discontentment or tired of the struggle questions might be more helpful.

1. What were you expecting to gain/accomplish/achieve?

2. What happened instead?

3. Based on your past experiences with projects and goals, does success usually come in a nice, neat, always-moving-upward curve? If not, how does it usually come?

4. Do you think this is just a minor setback or is it the death of your project? Explain.

5. What will you need to do if you want to be successful with this project?

6. What do you think God wants to teach you through this trial?

7. Is there anything you need to accept?

8. Is there anything you need to trust God with?

9. What can you thank God for in this situation? See verses below for ideas.

Bible Verses

Isaiah 40:28-31 Do you not know? Have you not heard? The Everlasting God, the Lord, the Creator of the ends of the earth does not become weary or tired. His understanding is inscrutable. He gives strength to the weary, and to him who lacks might He increases power. Though youths grow weary and tired, and vigorous young men stumble badly, yet those who wait for the Lord will gain new strength; they will mount up with wings like eagles, they will run and not get tired, they will walk and not become weary.

Psalm 30:5b Weeping may last for the night, but a shout of joy comes in the morning.

Psalm 62:5-8 My soul, wait in silence for God only, for my hope is from Him. He only is my rock and my salvation, my stronghold; I shall not be shaken. On God my salvation and my glory rest; the rock of my strength, my refuge is in God. Trust in Him at all times, O people; pour out your heart before Him; God is a refuge for us. Selah.

Lamentations 3:22-23 The Lord's lovingkindnesses indeed never cease, for his compassions never fail. They are new every morning; great is Your faithfulness.

Romans 8:28 And we know that God causes all things to work together for good to those who love God, to those who are called according to His purpose.

Philippians 4:6-7 Be anxious for nothing, but in everything by prayer and supplication with thanksgiving let your requests be made known to God. And the peace of God, which surpasses all comprehension, will guard your hearts and your minds in Christ Jesus.

See also: tired of the struggle, discontentment, perfectionism, and lack of confidence.

Dread

1. What would you like to accomplish today? Be specific.

2. Why do you want to accomplish that?

3. Why don't you feel like working right now?

4. What do you feel like doing instead?

5. If you ignore your project and do that instead, how will you feel afterwards?

6. What will you have to sacrifice to work on your project?

7. How will you feel when you complete this project and why will you feel that way?

8. When you think of how you'll feel, is it worth the sacrifice to work on it?

9. What's the first thing you need to do if you want to work on this project? (Example: Get out your notebook, open the computer file, look up the telephone number, etc.)

10. Why don't you do that right now and see how it goes from there?

Bible Verses

Psalm 61:1-4 Hear my cry, O God; give heed to my prayer. From the end of the earth I call to You when my heart is faint; lead me to the rock that is higher than I. For You have been a refuge for me, a tower of strength against the enemy. Let me dwell in your tent forever; let me take refuge in the shelter of Your wings.

Psalm 68:35 O God, You are awesome from Your sanctuary. The God of Israel Himself gives strength and power to the people. Blessed be God!

Jonah 2:9a But I will sacrifice to You with the voice of thanksgiving.

2 Corinthians 12:9a And He has said to me, "My grace is sufficient for you, for power is perfected in weakness."

Hebrews 12:11 All discipline for the moment seems not to be joyful, but sorrowful; yet to those who have been trained by it, afterwards it yields the peaceful fruit of righteousness.

See also: procrastination, beginning of day stress, indulgence, perfectionism, and lack of confidence.

Entitlement

1. Why do you feel like you shouldn't have to work on your goal (habit, list) right now?

2. Why do you feel like you *should* work on it right now?

3. Do you think God wants you to work on your habit or goal right now? Why or why not?

    a. **Yes:** If so, what sacrifices will you have to make to do what God wants you to do? Do you love Him enough to make those sacrifices?

    b. **No:** If not, what do you think God wants you to do instead? Why don't you skip the rest of these questions and go do that?

    c. **God doesn't care:** Would you rather do something else or accomplish your goal, knowing that you can't do both?

4. Is it possible to accomplish this goal (or develop this habit) without ever making any sacrifices for it?

5. What are the advantages of accomplishing this goal (or developing this habit)? List as many as possible.

6. When you think of all the advantages, is it worth the sacrifice to work on it?

Bible Verses

Galatians 5:13 For you were called to freedom, brethren; only do not turn your freedom into an opportunity for the flesh, but through love serve one another.

Colossians 3:17 Whatever you do in word or deed, do all in the name of the Lord Jesus, giving thanks through Him to God the Father.

Hebrews 10:36 For you have need of endurance, so that when you have done the will of God, you may receive what was promised.

1 John 3:16 We know love by this, that He laid down His life for us; and we ought to lay down our lives for the brethren.

See also: discontentment and indulgence.

Failure

1. Is it possible to follow your plan (to-do list) perfectly every single day? Why or why not?

2. Why do you think you got off track today?

3. Since you can't go back and change the past, what do you think God wants you to do now?

   a. Be an all or nothing person. If you can't follow your plan perfectly, don't follow it at all.

   b. Beat yourself up and think about what a loser you are.

   c. Keep telling yourself, "You should follow your plan!" Then ignore yourself and go do something else.

   d. Do something else worthwhile that's *not* on the list so that at least you won't feel quite so guilty.

   e. Recognize that things don't always go as expected. Accept the fact that you got sidetracked. Remember that life is about loving God and others, not about performing perfectly. Get back to work on your list/goal, thanking Him that you still have time to work on it.

4. What would be the advantage of continuing to work on your goal (list) even if things haven't gone as smoothly as you wanted them to go?

5. When you think of what you'll gain, is it worth the sacrifice to follow your plan (list) the rest of the day?

6. What can you thank God for in this situation?

Bible Verses

Isaiah 43:18-19 Do not call to mind the former things, or ponder things of the past. Behold, I will do something new, now it will spring forth; will you not be aware of it? I will even make a roadway in the wilderness, rivers in the desert.

Joshua 1:9 Have I not commanded you? Be strong and courageous! Do not tremble or be dismayed, for the Lord your God is with you wherever you go.

2 Corinthians 5:17 Therefore if anyone is in Christ, he is a new creature; the old things passed away; behold, new things have come.

Philippians 4:13 I can do all things through Him who strengthens me.

Hebrews 12:1-2a Therefore, since we have so great a cloud of witnesses surrounding us, let us also lay aside every encumbrance and the sin which so easily entangles us, and let us run with endurance the race that is set before us, fixing our eyes on Jesus, the author and perfecter of faith.

See also: perfectionism, beginning of day stress, and self-condemnation.

Fear of Condemnation

1. Who specifically do you think will make fun of you or condemn you? Name names. *

2. For each person on your list, answer the following questions:

   a. Is this person an accepting, positive, encouraging person by nature? If not, what type of person is he?

   b. Does this person agree with what you're doing? If not, how does he feel about it?

   c. Given this person's personality and priorities, do you think it's realistic to expect him to be positive about your project? Why or why not?

   d. If this person doesn't value your project does that mean your project isn't valuable? If not, what does it mean?

3. Do you think God wants you to press on with this project even though you might be criticized? Why or why not?

4. What will you need to accept if you decide to press on with this project?

5. What do you think God wants to teach you through this trial?

6. What can you thank Him for in this situation?

* **Note:** If you're more concerned with the general mass of people out there rather than individuals, direct your questions toward the general population.

Bible Verses

Psalm 27:1, 3-5 The Lord is my light and my salvation; whom shall I fear? The Lord is the defense of my life; whom shall I dread? Though a host encamp against me, my heart will not fear; though war arise against me, in spite of this I shall be confident. One thing I have asked from the Lord, that I shall seek: that I may dwell in the house of the Lord all the days of my life, to behold the beauty of the Lord and to meditate in His temple. For in the day of trouble He will conceal me in His tabernacle; in the secret place of His tent He will hide me; He will lift me up on a rock.

Psalm 56:4 In God, whose word I praise, in God I have put my trust; I shall not be afraid. What can mere man do to me?

Galatians 1:10 For am I now seeking the favor of men, or of God? Or am I striving to please men? If I were still trying to please men, I would not be a bond-servant of Christ.

2 Timothy 1:7-9 For God has not given us a spirit of timidity, but of power and love and discipline. Therefore do not be ashamed of the testimony of our Lord or of me His prisoner, but join with me in suffering for the gospel according to the power of God, who has saved us and called us with a holy calling, not according to our works, but according to His own purpose and grace which was granted us in Christ Jesus from all eternity.

See also: insecurity/feeling inadequate, people pleasing, social situations, and worry.

Fear of Failure

If you're afraid of failure because...

1. **People will make fun of you:** see fear of condemnation.

2. **You're afraid you won't be rewarded for your efforts:** see reward/ obsession.

3. **You think you're incapable of succeeding:** see lack of confidence.

4. **You feel like you have to succeed:** see greed/lust, reward/obsession, or the questions below.

5. **If you're not sure why you're afraid:** see worry/fear or the questions below.

Fear of Failure

1. What would you like to accomplish?

2. What are the odds of you being able to accomplish that? Explain.

3. Why do you want to accomplish that goal?

4. Do you think God also wants you to achieve that goal?

   a. **Yes:** If so, why does He want you to accomplish it?

   b. **No:** If not, what does He want?

5. Are God's priorities different than yours? Explain.

6. What are you most afraid of?

7. Why are you afraid of that?

8. Are you coming from a place of being filled up with God and finding your worth in Him? If not, what do you think you have to

have to be happy and worthy (success, approval of others, security, status, wealth, etc.)?

9. Would God agree with you? If not, what would He say?

10. What can you thank God for in this situation?

11. Is there anything you need to accept?

Bible Verses

Isaiah 41:9-10 You whom I have taken from the ends of the earth, and called from its remotest parts and said to you, 'You are my servant, I have chosen you and not rejected you.' 'Do not fear, for I am with you; do not anxiously look about you, for I am your God. I will strengthen you, surely I will help you, surely I will uphold you with My righteous right hand.'

Jeremiah 17:7 Blessed is the man who trusts in the Lord and whose trust is the Lord.

Jeremiah 29:11 "For I know the plans I have for you," declares the Lord, "plans for welfare and not for calamity to give you a future and a hope."

Philippians 4:19 And my God will supply all your needs according to His riches in glory in Christ Jesus.

Philippians 3:8 More than that, I count all things to be loss in view of the surpassing value of knowing Christ Jesus my Lord, for whom I have suffered the loss of all things, and count them but rubbish so that I may gain Christ.

Philippians 1:21 For to me, to live is Christ and to die is gain.

See also: fear of condemnation, reward/obsession, greed/lust, and worry.

Indulgence

1. What would you like to accomplish today? Be specific.

2. Why do you want to accomplish that?

3. What do you feel like doing instead?

4. On a scale of 1 to 10, how satisfying do you think that would be? Explain.

5. In the past, have you been able to do what you feel like doing and still accomplish your goals? Why or why not?

6. What are the advantages of working on your goal (to-do list), even when you don't feel like working on it?

7. Are goals easy to accomplish, or do you usually have to give up something to accomplish them?

8. What will you need to give up to accomplish your goal (or follow your list) this time?

9. When you think of all you'll accomplish, is it worth the sacrifice?

Bible Verses

Ephesians 5:15-17 Therefore be careful how you walk, not as unwise men but as wise, making the most of your time, because the days are evil. So then do not be foolish, but understand what the will of the Lord is.

Romans 13:14 But put on the Lord Jesus Christ, and make no provision for the flesh in regard to its lusts.

1 Peter 1:14-16 As obedient children, do not be conformed to the former lusts which were yours in your ignorance, but like the Holy One who called you, be holy yourselves also in all your behavior, because it is written, "You shall be holy, for I am holy."

1 John 2:15-16 Do not love the world not the things in the world. If anyone loves the world, the love of the Father is not in him. For all that is in the world, the lust of the flesh and the lust of the eyes and the boastful pride of life, is not from the Father, but is from the world.

See also: dread, entitlement, procrastination, and greed/lust.

Justification

1. What are you supposed to be doing?

2. Why do you feel like there's a good reason not to do that right now? Be specific.

3. Is that really a good reason for not working on your goal? Why or why not?

   a. **Yes:** If so, is there anything you can do now to make it easier to get back to work later? Go ahead and do that and enjoy the time off. You don't need to answer the rest of these questions.

   b. **No:** Is it always convenient to work on goals? What will you have to give up to work on your goal today?

4. What will you gain if you work on your goal, even when it's hard?

5. When you think of what you'll gain, is it worth the sacrifice?

6. What do you think God wants to teach you through this trial?

7. What can you thank God for in this situation?

Bible Verses

Colossians 3:23-24 Whatever you do, do your work heartily, as for the Lord rather than for men, knowing that from the Lord you will receive the reward of the inheritance. It is the Lord Christ whom you serve.

1 Corinthians 6:12 All things are lawful for me, but not all things are profitable. All things are lawful for me, but I will not be mastered by anything.

1 Thessalonians 5:21 But examine everything carefully; hold fast to that which is good.

See also: lack of time or perfect conditions and lack of importance.

Lack of Confidence

1. What would you like to do?

2. Why do you want to do that?

3. Are you one of those rare (or possibly non-existent) people who can do this effortlessly and perfectly right from the beginning? If not, what's the sad truth you'll have to accept?

4. Has God given you any gifts, talents, or character traits that will make it easier to reach your goal? If so, what are they?

5. What will you need to do if you want to reach your goal? Be specific.

6. Will you have to do that alone, or do you think God would be willing to help? Explain.

7. What do you think God wants to teach you through this trial?

8. What will you gain if you turn to Him for help with this project?

9. What will you gain if you procrastinate, obsess, or turn to a bad habit for "help" with this project?

10. Do you want that to happen?

11. If not, what do you need to do to protect yourself?

12. What is the first task you need to do to get this project going? Be specific. (Example: Get out your notebook, open the computer file, look up the telephone number, etc.)

13. Why don't you do that right now and see how it goes from there?

Note: I debated about what Bible verses to put in this category because I don't want to imply that we can do anything we set our minds to do. After all, God's in control, not us, and He may not want us to accomplish some of the goals we set out to achieve. Thankfully, He's much better at being in control than we are! As you pray through the Bible verses below, keep in mind that some verses will only apply if you're working on a goal that God wants you to accomplish.

Bible Verses

Psalm 18:29 For by You I can run upon a troop; and by my God I can leap over a wall.

Jeremiah 32:27 Behold, I am the Lord, the God of all flesh; is anything too difficult for me?

Jeremiah 32:17 Ah Lord God! Behold, You have made the heavens and the earth by Your great power and by your outstretched arm! Nothing is too difficult for you.

Zechariah 4:6b "Not by might nor by power, but by My Spirit," says the Lord of hosts.

2 Corinthians 12:9 And He has said to me, "My grace is sufficient for you, for power is perfected in weakness." Most gladly, therefore, I will rather boast about my weaknesses, so that the power of Christ may dwell in me.

Philippians 4:13 I can do all things through Him who strengthens me.

Philippians 4:19 And my God will supply all your needs according to His riches in glory in Christ Jesus.

See also: dread, disappointment, beginning of day stress, fear of failure, and perfectionism.

Lack of Importance

1. Why do you feel like it's not a big deal if you don't work on your project (or habit) today?

2. If you decide to take the day off, will you be more inclined to take the day off tomorrow as well? Why or why not?

3. Why do you want to develop this habit or accomplish this goal?

4. Do you think God wants you to develop this habit or accomplish this goal? Why or why not?

   a. **Yes:** If so, what will you need to sacrifice to do what He wants you to do?

   b. **No:** If not, what's driving you to work on this project? What would you have to sacrifice to give up this project?

   c. **God doesn't care:** Why would you like to finish this project or accomplish this goal? What will you need to sacrifice to accomplish your goal?

5. Is starting this habit (or achieving this goal) worth the sacrifice? Why or why not?

6. Is it worth the sacrifice even on days you don't feel like working on it?

7. What will happen if you're not willing to make that sacrifice?

8. Do you want that to happen?

9. If you want to develop this habit (or reach this goal), will you eventually have to make the sacrifice to work on it?

10. If so, what would be the advantage of getting started right now?

11. What do you think God wants to teach you through this trial?

12. What can you thank Him for?

Note: I don't have any general Bible verses for this category because from a biblical perspective not all projects are important. I would have a hard time coming up with Bible verses for organizing my closet, for example, because I don't think God cares if I organize it. If you feel like God wants you to work on your habit or goal, find some Bible verses that are specific to your particular project. Use the following Bible verses if you're trying to start a quiet time habit or a renewing of the mind habit.

Bible Verses

Psalm 27:8 When You said, "Seek My face," my heart said to You, "Your face, O Lord, I shall seek."

Jeremiah 29:13 You will seek Me and find Me when you search for Me with all your heart.

Hosea 6:3 So let us know, let us press on to know the Lord. His going forth is as certain as the dawn; and He will come to us like the rain, like the spring rain watering the earth.

Zechariah 2:10 Sing for joy and be glad, O daughter of Zion; for behold I am coming and I will dwell in your midst.

John 8:31-32 So Jesus was saying to those Jews who had believed Him, "If you continue in My word, then you are truly disciples of Mine; and you will know the truth, and the truth will make you free."

John 14:26 But the Helper, the Holy Spirit, whom the Father will send in My name, He will teach you all things, and bring to your remembrance all that I said to you.

John 15:4-5 Abide in Me, and I in you. As the branch cannot bear fruit of itself unless it abides in the vine, so neither can you unless you abide in Me. I am the vine, you are the branches; he who abides in Me and I in him, he bears much fruit, for apart from Me you can do nothing.

Romans 12:2 And do not be conformed to this world, but be transformed by the renewing of your mind, so that you may prove what the will of God is, that which is good and acceptable and perfect.

See also: indulgence, justification, and lack of time.

Lack of Time or
Perfect Conditions

1. Why do you feel like you can't work on your goal or to-do list today?

2. How much time would it take to do it?

3. Which of the following is true:

    a. You really don't have time to work on it.

    b. You could make the time, but you'd rather not. *

    c. You dread the thought of working on your goal or to-do list, and time is a good excuse. *

    d. You feel like you need the perfect conditions to work on it and conditions aren't ideal right now.

4. Is life always perfect, or do you sometimes have to make do and adjust your plans?

5. Is this one of those days where you'll have to adjust your plans if you want to accomplish your goal? Explain.

6. Think of the day ahead. When can you fit in time to work on your goal or to-do list?

7. Would you like to make a new plan to do that? If so, what is your plan?

8. What will happen if you consistently put off this project when conditions aren't perfect?

9. What would be the value of working on it today even though conditions aren't perfect?

10. Is there anything you need to accept?

*If this is true, determine the real reason you don't want to work on your project and use one of the other sets of questions to renew your mind.

Bible Verses

Psalm 90:12 So teach us to number our days, that we may present to You a heart of wisdom.

Ephesians 5:15-17 Look carefully then how you walk, not as unwise but as wise, making the best use of the time, because the days are evil. Therefor do not be foolish, but understand what the will of the Lord is.

Colossians 3:23-24 Whatever you do, do your work heartily, as for the Lord rather than for men, knowing that from the Lord you will receive the reward of the inheritance. It is the Lord Christ whom you serve.

1 Thessalonians 5:6 So then let us not sleep as others do, but let us be alert and sober.

See also: beginning of day stress, end of day stress, and lack of time (extreme version).

Lack of Time
(Extreme Version)

1. Is there anything special going on in your life right now that's keeping you from spending time on your goal?

   a. **Yes:** If so, do you think God wants you to put your goal off until later? Why or why not?

   b. **No:** If not, continue on with the questions.

2. In the past 48 hours, how much time have you spent in the following activities? Be specific.

   a. Facebook

   b. YouTube

   c. Television

   d. Texting

   e. Computer games

   f. Hobbies

   g. Recreational activities

   h. Hanging out with friends

   i. Surfing the Internet

   j. Exercise

   k. Reading

   l. Talking on the phone

   m. Wandering around your house or apartment

   n. Work that isn't required to support you or your family

3. Would it be possible to make some time for your goal by cutting down on some of your other activities?

4. If so, what could you cut out of your schedule to allow time for your habit or goal?

5. Is there any reason you couldn't start working on your goal right now?

6. If not, why don't you go ahead and get started?

Note: See lack of time/perfect conditions questions for Bible verses.

See also: beginning of day stress and end of day stress questions and Bible verses.

Perfectionism

1. What are you trying to do perfectly?

2. What would perfection look like in this case? (Give a thorough description.)

3. Are you capable of making that happen? (Be realistic.)

4. Why do you feel like you have to be perfect?

5. Are you believing any lies? If so, what's the truth for each lie?

6. Does God think you have to be perfect? Why or why not?

7. How is your perfectionism affecting the following:

    a. Your project or habit

    b. Your relationship with God

    c. Your relationship with others

    d. Your health

    e. Your personal well-being

8. Is your pursuit of "perfect" worth the sacrifice? Why or why not?

9. What would it look like to pursue this goal as a non-perfectionist?

10. Would you like to pursue this goal as a non-perfectionist? Why or why not?

11. Is there anything you need to accept?

12. What can you thank God for in this situation?

Bible Verses

Matthew 11:28-30 Come to Me, all who are weary and heavy-laden, and I will give you rest. Take My yoke upon you and learn from Me, for I am gentle and humble in heart, and you will find rest for your souls. For My yoke is easy and My burden is light.

Luke 10:41-42 But the Lord answered and said to her, "Martha, Martha, you are worried and bothered about so many things; but only one thing is necessary, for Mary has chosen the good part, which shall not be taken away from her."

John 8:10-11 Straightening up, Jesus said to her, "Woman, where are they? Did no one condemn you?" She said, "No one, Lord." And Jesus said, "I do not condemn you, either. Go. From now on sin no more."

Romans 8:28 And we know that God causes all things to work together for good to those who love God, to those who are called according to His purpose.

2 Corinthians 12:9 And He has said to me, "My grace is sufficient for you, for power is perfected in weakness." Most gladly, therefore, I will rather boast about my weaknesses, so that the power of Christ may dwell in me.

Hebrews 4:15-16 For we do not have a high priest who cannot sympathize with our weaknesses, but One who has been tempted in all things as we are, yet without sin. Therefore let us draw near with confidence to the throne of grace, so that we may receive mercy and find grace to help in time of need.

See also: reward/obsession, greed/lust, self-condemnation, feeling inadequate, people pleasing, end of day stress, workaholism, frustration, and worry.

Procrastination

1. What would you like to accomplish? Be specific.

2. Why don't you want to work on it right now?

3. Based on past experience, what usually happens when you tell yourself you'll do a job later?

4. If you put this off now, when do you think you'll end up doing it? (Be honest.)

5. In the long run, is the procrastination life the good life? Why or why not?

6. If you want to finish this job, will you eventually have to make the sacrifice to work on it?

7. What would you gain by doing it right now?

8. What's the first thing you need to do if you want to work on this project? (Example: Get out your notebook, open the computer file, look up the telephone number, etc.)

9. Why don't you do that right now and see how it goes from there?

Note: If the job seems overwhelming, try breaking it into smaller steps. Each step should be fairly easy and non-intimidating. After breaking it into steps, block the whole project from your mind and focus on one step at a time.

Bible Verses

Psalm 18:29 For by You I can run upon a troop; and by my God I can leap over a wall.

Jeremiah 42:6b Whether it is pleasant or unpleasant, we will listen to the voice of the Lord our God.

Philippians 4:13 I can do all things through Him who strengthens me.

Philippians 4:19 And my God will supply all your needs according to His riches in glory in Christ Jesus.

Colossians 3:17 Whatever you do in word or deed, do all in the name of the Lord Jesus, giving thanks through Him to God the Father.

Hebrews 10:36 For you have need of endurance, so that when you have done the will of God, you may receive what was promised.

Hebrews 12:11 All discipline for the moment seems not to be joyful, but sorrowful; yet to those who have been trained by it, afterwards it yields the peaceful fruit of righteousness.

See also: dread, perfectionism, fear of failure, and beginning of day stress.

Reward/Obsession

1. What is your goal?

2. What will you need to do to accomplish your goal? Be specific.

3. How would you define success with this project?

4. Is it a given that if you do what you need to do, you'll be successful? Why or why not?

5. If you decide to pursue this project, what will you need to accept?

6. Do you think God wants you to work on this project? Why or why not?

7. How do you think He would define success with this project?

8. Is God's definition of success easier to achieve than yours? Why or why not?

9. What would be the advantage of going to God for help with this project, including going to Him for help to see the project through His eyes?

10. Which would be a better reward: 1) intense fellowship with God as you go to Him for help and keep Him (rather than the project) first in your life or 2) money, recognition, and/or worldly success with the project? Explain.

11. What sacrifices will you have to make to get the better reward?

12. Are God's lessons and love in the midst of a trial a reward in and of themselves?

13. What can you thank God for in this situation?

Bible Verses

Habakkuk 3:17-19 Though the fig tree should not blossom and there be no fruit on the vines, though the yield of the olive should fail and the fields produce no food, though the flock should be cut off from the fold and there be no cattle in the stalls, yet I will exult in the Lord, I will rejoice in the God of my salvation. The Lord God is my strength, and He has made my feet like hinds' feet, and makes me walk on my high places.

Matthew 11:28-30 Come to Me, all who are weary and heavy-laden, and I will give you rest. Take My yoke upon you and learn from Me, for I am gentle and humble in heart, and you will find rest for your souls. For My yoke is easy and My burden is light.

John 6:27 Do not work for the food which perishes, but for the food which endures to eternal life, which the Son of Man will give to you, for on Him the Father, God, has set His seal.

Matthew 6:24, 33 No one can serve two masters; for either he will hate the one and love the other, or he will be devoted to one and despise the other. You cannot serve God and wealth. But seek first His kingdom and His righteousness, and all these things will be added to you.

James 1:16, 17 Do not be deceived, my beloved brethren. Every good thing given and every perfect gift is from above, coming down from the Father of lights, with whom there is no variation or shifting shadow.

See also: greed/lust, fear of failure, workaholism, and worry.

Social Media/Stats/Emails

1. Why do you want to know how many people are (liking your Facebook statuses, visiting your blog, following you, emailing you, etc.)?

2. Will a high number really tell you what you want to know? Why or why not?

3. How will you feel if the number isn't as high as you want it to be?

4. What are the chances the numbers will be as high as you want them to be?

5. How does your frequent checking affect the following:

   a. Your personal wellbeing

   b. Your productivity

   c. Your relationship with God

   d. Your project or goal

6. Do you think God wants you to have boundaries in this area of your life? Why or why not?

7. What will you gain if you follow your boundaries in this area of your life?

8. When you think of all you'll gain, is it worth the sacrifice?

Bible Verses

Matthew 6:1 Beware of practicing your righteousness before men to be noticed by them; otherwise you have no reward with your Father who is in heaven.

Matthew 6:33 But seek first His kingdom and His righteousness, and all these things will be added to you.

Galatians 1:10 For am I now seeking the favor of men, or of God? Or am I striving to please men? If I were still trying to please men, I would not be a bond-servant of Christ.

Philippians 2:4 Do not merely look out for your own personal interests, but also for the interests of others.

Philippians 4:11-13 Not that I speak from want, for I have learned to be content in whatever circumstances I am. I know how to get along with humble means, and I also know how to live in prosperity; in any and every circumstance I have learned the secret of being filled and going hungry, both of having abundance and suffering need. I can do all things through Him who strengthens me.

See also: reward/obsession, greed/lust, fear of failure, feeling inadequate, and people pleasing.

Workaholism

1. Why do you feel like you should work right now?

2. Why do you feel like you *shouldn't* work right now?

3. Do you think God wants you to work right now? Why or why not?

4. If not, what sacrifices will you have to make to do what God wants you to do?

5. Is it worth doing what God wants you to do even if it's inconvenient or costly? Why or why not?

6. List the advantages of taking a break from both work and thinking about work for awhile.

7. When you think of the advantages, in terms of both life and your relationship with God, is it really that much of a sacrifice to take a break from work?

Bible Verses

Psalm 46:10 Cease striving and know that I am God; I will be exalted among the nations, I will be exalted in the earth.

Philippians 3:7-8 But whatever things were gain to me, those things I have counted as loss for the sake of Christ. More than that, I count all things to be loss in view of the surpassing value of knowing Christ Jesus my Lord, for whom I have suffered the loss of all things, and count them but rubbish so that I may gain Christ.

Colossians 3:1-3 Therefore if you have been raised up with Christ, keep seeking the things above, where Christ is, seated at the right hand of God. Set your mind on the things above, not on the things that are on earth. For you have died and your life is hidden with Christ in God.

Hebrews 12:1-2a Therefore, since we have so great a cloud of witnesses surrounding us, let us also lay aside every encumbrance and the sin which so easily entangles us, and let us run with endurance the race that is set before us, fixing our eyes on Jesus, the author and perfecter of faith.

See also: greed/lust/idolatry, insecurity/people pleasing, perfectionism, end of workday stress, fear of failure, worry, and reward/obsession.

LETTING GO OF
NEGATIVE
EMOTIONS

```
QUESTIONS
AND
BIBLE VERSES
```

Anger and Annoyance

1. Why are you annoyed? Be specific.

2. Are you surprised by this person's behavior? Why or why not?

3. Why does her behavior bother you so much?

4. Do you think her behavior bothers God? Why or why not?

5. Do you think this person is open to change?

    a. **Yes:** If so, do you think God wants you to talk to her? Why or why not? *

    b. **No:** If not, what will happen if you try to change a person who doesn't want to be changed?

6. How do you think God wants you to respond to this person?

7. What would you need to give up, if anything, to respond the way God wants you to respond?

8. Do you love God (or this person) enough to make that sacrifice?

9. Is there anything you need to accept?

10. What do you think God wants to do for you in the midst of this difficult situation? (See insecurity verses for ideas.)

11. Do you need to add some boundaries to this relationship? If so, what boundaries could you actually enforce? **

12. What can you thank God for in this situation? (Don't forget to include the things you like about this person.)

* If you think God wants you to talk to this person, try renewing your mind first so your heart is full of love and respect for her. You'll have a better chance of reaching her if she doesn't feel threatened by your anger or condemnation.

** If this relationship is abusive or potentially abusive, please get help as soon as possible.

Possible things you'll need to accept: that people don't always do what you want them to do, that you don't have the power to change people, that you can't always have what you want, and that life is often unfair.

Possible things you'll need to confess: trying to control people God doesn't want you to control, making something more important than God wants you to make it, hurting others with your anger, and judging and condemning others.

Bible Verses

Matthew 5:43-44, 46 You have heard that it was said, "You shall love your neighbor and hate your enemy." But I say to you, love your enemies and pray for those who persecute you. For if you love those who love you, what reward do you have? Do not even the tax collectors do the same?

Matthew 18:21-22 Then Peter came to Jesus and asked, "Lord, how many times shall I forgive my brother or sister who sins against me? Up to seven times?" Jesus answered, "I tell you, not seven times, but seventy-seven times."

Ephesians 4:26-27 Be angry and yet do not sin; do not let the sun go down on your anger, and do not give the devil an opportunity.

Romans 12:18 If possible, so far as it depends on you, be at peace with all men.

Romans 15:1, 7 Now we who are strong ought to bear the weaknesses of those without strength and not just please ourselves. Each of us is to please his neighbor for his good, to his edification. Therefore, accept one another, just as Christ also accepted us to the glory of God.

1 Corinthians 13:4-5, 7 Love is patient, love is kind and is not jealous; love does not brag and is not arrogant, does not act unbecomingly; it does not seek its own, is not provoked, does not take into account a wrong suffered. (Love) bears all things, believes all things, hopes all things, endures all things.

Colossians 3:12-15 So, as those who have been chosen of God, holy and beloved, put on a heart of compassion, kindness, humility, gentleness and patience; bearing with one another, and forgiving each other, whoever has a complaint against anyone; just as the Lord forgave you, so also should you. Beyond all these things put on love, which is the perfect bond of unity. Let the peace of Christ rule in your hearts, to which indeed you were called in one body; and be thankful.

Colossians 3:17 Whatever you do in word or deed, do all in the name of the Lord Jesus, giving thanks through Him to God the Father.

1 Peter 1:22 Since you have in obedience to the truth purified your souls for a sincere love of the brethren, fervently love one another from the heart.

1 Peter 3:8-9 To sum up, all of you be harmonious, sympathetic, brotherly, kindhearted, and humble in spirit; not returning evil for evil or insult for insult, but giving a blessing instead; for you were called for the very purpose that you might inherit a blessing.

Note: As you pray through these verses, pray for the person who is bugging you. God will change your heart as you pray for him or her.

See also: discontentment, frustration, insecurity, judgment, pride, and worry.

Discontentment, Boredom, and Loneliness

1. Why are you unhappy (bored or lonely)?

2. What do you think will make you happy?

3. Will that really make you happy? Why or why not?

4. Are you able to create the conditions you think will make you happy?

    a. **Yes:** If so, do you think God wants you to work on that? Why or why not?

    b. **No:** If not, is there anything else you can do to make life better? Explain.

5. Is God enough to satisfy you, even if you don't get what you want?

6. What is one thing you can do to draw closer to Him today?

7. What is one thing you can do to show love to others today? Be specific.

8. Is there anything you need to accept?

9. Is there anything you need to hold with open hands?

10. Is there anything God wants you to do?

11. What can you thank God for in this situation?

Possible things you'll need to accept with boredom: that life isn't always fun and exciting and that sometimes you have to give up fun and excitement to love others well.

Possible things you'll need to accept with loneliness: that people don't always love you the way you want to be loved, that people sometimes leave when you don't want them to leave, that it can be hard to make friends, and that you might have to be the one to make the first move if you want more friends.

Possible things you may need to accept with discontentment: that life doesn't always go the way you want it to go, that people don't always do what you want them to do, that God calls you to love even when it's not easy or fun to love, and that God calls you to be thankful even when you don't feel like being thankful.

Possible things you'll need to confess with boredom, discontentment, and loneliness: that you're making something more important than God wants you to make it, that you're not holding all things with open hands, that you're relying on people and things to get your needs met instead of relying on God, that you're expecting others to reach out to you rather than you reaching out to others, and that you have a demanding spirit.

Bible Verses

Psalm 43:5 Why are you downcast, O my soul? Why so disturbed within me? Put your hope in God, for I will yet praise him, my Savior and my God. (NIV)

Psalm 73:25 Whom have I in heaven but You? And besides You, I desire nothing on earth.

Jonah 2:9a But I will sacrifice to You with the voice of thanksgiving.

Jeremiah 31:9-11 "With weeping they will come, and by supplication I will lead them; I will make them walk by streams of waters, on a straight path in which they will not stumble; for I am a father to Israel, and Ephraim is My firstborn." Hear the word of the Lord, O nations, and declare in the coastlands afar off, and say, "He who scattered Israel will gather him and keep him as a shepherd keeps his flock." For the Lord has ransomed Jacob and redeemed him from the hand of him who was stronger than he.

Jeremiah 31:13b-14 "For I will turn their mourning into joy and will comfort them and give them joy for their sorrow. I will fill the souls of the priests with abundance, and My people will be satisfied with My goodness," declares the Lord.

Philippians 4:6-8 Be anxious for nothing, but in everything by prayer and supplication with thanksgiving let your requests be made known to God. And the peace of God, which surpasses all comprehension, will guard your hearts and your minds in Christ Jesus. Finally, brethren, whatever is true, whatever is honorable, whatever is right, whatever is pure, whatever is lovely, whatever is of good repute, if there is any excellence and if anything worthy of praise, dwell on these things.

Philippians 4:11-13 Not that I speak from want, for I have learned to be content in whatever circumstances I am. I know how to get along with humble means, and I also know how to live in prosperity; in any and every circumstance I have learned the secret of being filled and going hungry, both of having abundance and suffering need. I can do all things through Him who strengthens me.

1 Timothy 6:6-8 But godliness actually is a means of great gain when accompanied by contentment. For we have brought nothing into the world, so we cannot take anything out of it either. If we have food and covering, with these we shall be content.

1 John 3:16 We know love by this, that He laid down His life for us; and we ought to lay down our lives for the brethren.

See also: anger, boredom (starting and stopping a habit), disappointment (starting a habit), despair (stopping a habit), frustration, insecurity, procrastination, and worry.

Envy

1. Why are envious of this person?

2. Are you capable of getting what she has?

   a. **Yes:** If so, what would you have to do to get it? Are you willing to do that? Does God want you to do that? Why or why not?

   b. **No:** If not, do you have blessings that she doesn't have? Explain.

3. Could God give you what she has if He wanted to?

4. Can you think of any reason He might not want to?

5. Is God enough to satisfy you even if you don't get what you want?

6. Is there anything you need to accept?

7. Is there anything you need to confess?

8. What can you thank God for in this situation?

Possible things you'll need to accept: that you don't always get what you want, that you don't always get what others have, that you don't always get what you feel like you deserve, and that life in general isn't fair.

Possible things you'll need to confess: that you're resenting or judging those who have more than you, that you're not being thankful for what you have, that you're not learning how to be content in all situations, and that you're not making life about God.

Bible Verses

Luke 12:15 Then (Jesus) said to them, "Beware, and be on your guard against every form of greed; for not even when one has an abundance does his life consist of possessions."

Philippians 4:11-13 Not that I speak from want, for I have learned to be content in whatever circumstances I am. I know how to get along with humble means, and I also know how to live in prosperity; in any and every circumstance I have learned the secret of being filled and going hungry, both of having abundance and suffering need. I can do all things through Him who strengthens me.

1 Thessalonians 5:18 In everything give thanks; for this is God's will for you in Christ Jesus.

1 John 2:15-16 Do not love the world nor the things in the world. If anyone loves the world, the love of the Father is not in him. For all that is in the world, the lust of the flesh and the lust of the eyes and the boastful pride of life, is not from the Father, but is from the world.

See also: anger, discontentment, judgment, and pride.

Frustration

Note: If you're frustrated with something you can't change, use the discontentment questions.

1. Why are you frustrated?

2. Based on your past experiences with life (work, relationships, diets, etc.), are you surprised that things aren't going smoothly? Why or why not?

3. Are you expecting life to be easy, or are you accepting the fact that life is often difficult, inefficient, and messy?

4. Are you expecting everyone to co-operate with your plans, or are you remembering that they have their own lives with their own plans?

5. Do you think God wants you to keep working on this project even though it's hard?

   a. **Yes:** If so, what will you need to give up to do what God wants you to do?

   b. **No:** If not, what will you need to give up to do what God wants you to do?

   c. **God doesn't care:** Is this project worth the hassle and effort? Why or why not?

6. Is there anything you need to accept?

7. What can you thank God for in this situation?

Possible things you'll need to accept: that life doesn't always go smoothly, that God often asks us to do hard things, that people don't always cooperate with our plans, and that life is often inefficient, messy, and difficult.

Possible things you'll need to confess: a spoiled rich girl attitude, an unwillingness to work and suffer, a demanding spirit, self-absorption, laziness, judgment, anger, and arrogance.

Bible Verses

John 16:33 These things I (Jesus) have spoken to you, so that in Me you may have peace. In the world you have tribulation, but take courage: I have overcome the world.

2 Corinthians 4:16-17 Therefore we do not lose heart, but though our outer man is decaying, yet our inner man is being renewed day by day. For momentary, light affliction is producing for us an eternal weight of glory far beyond all comparison.

2 Corinthians 10:3-5 For though we walk in the flesh, we do not war according to the flesh, for the weapons of our warfare are not of the flesh, but divinely powerful for the destruction of fortresses. We are destroying speculations and every lofty thing raised up against the knowledge of God, and we are taking every thought captive to the obedience of Christ.

Ephesians 6:10-11 Finally, be strong in the Lord and in the strength of His might. Put on the full armor of God, so that you will be able to stand firm against the schemes of the devil.

Philippians 1:6 For I am confident of this very thing, that He who began a good work in you will perfect it until the day of Christ Jesus.

Philippians 4:11-13 Not that I speak from want, for I have learned to be content in whatever circumstances I am. I know how to get along with humble means, and I also know how to live in prosperity; in any and every circumstance I have learned the secret of being filled and going hungry, both of having abundance and suffering need. I can do all things through Him who strengthens me.

Hebrews 12:11 All discipline for the moment seems not to be joyful, but sorrowful; yet to those who have been trained by it, afterwards it yields the peaceful fruit of righteousness.

See also: anger, discontentment, disappointment (starting a habit), entitlement (starting a habit), and perfectionism.

Greed/Lust/Idolatry

1. What is it that you want? Be specific.

2. Why do you want that?

3. Do you think God wants that? If not, what does He want?

4. Are God's priorities different than your priorities? Explain.

5. What will happen if you clutch too tightly to what you want?

6. Do you want that to happen? If not, what will you need to do to protect yourself?

7. Is there anything you need to accept?

8. Is there anything you need to do?

Possible things you'll need to accept: that you'll never get enough to satisfy you if you're trying to fill yourself up with anything other than God.

Possible things you'll need to confess: making an idol of whatever it is that you want, impure motives and thoughts, not loving God with all your heart, soul, mind, and strength, and not loving your neighbor as yourself.

Bible Verses

Psalm 46:10 Cease striving and know that I am God; I will be exalted among the nations, I will be exalted in the earth.

Jeremiah 2:13 For My people have committed two evils: they have forsaken Me, the fountain of living waters, to hew for themselves cisterns, broken cisterns that can hold no water.

Luke 12:15 Then (Jesus) said to them, "Beware, and be on your guard against every form of greed; for not even when one has an abundance does his life consist of possessions."

Romans 13:14 But put on the Lord Jesus Christ, and make no provision for the flesh in regard to its lusts.

1 Corinthians 6:12 All things are lawful for me, but not all things are profitable. All things are lawful for me, but I will not be mastered by anything.

Philippians 3:7 But whatever things were gain to me, those things I have counted as loss for the sake of Christ.

Philippians 4:11 Not that I speak from want, for I have learned to be content in whatever circumstances I am.

Colossians 3:5 Therefore consider the members of your earthly body as dead to immorality, impurity, passion, evil desire, and greed, which amounts to idolatry.

Hebrews 12:1-2a Therefore, since we have so great a cloud of witnesses surrounding us, let us also lay aside every encumbrance and the sin which so easily entangles us, and let us run with endurance the race that is set before us, fixing our eyes on Jesus, the author and perfecter of faith.

See also: discontentment, envy, and reward/obsession.

Insecurity: Feeling Inadequate

1. Why do you think you're inadequate?

2. What do you think you have to do or have to be acceptable?

3. Are you capable of making that happen right now?

4. What do you look like when you see yourself through the eyes of the world and/or the eyes of your own expectations?

5. Is that how God sees you?

6. Who are you in God's eyes, and how does He feel about you? (Look at the verses below for ideas.)

7. How is God's view of you different than your own view or the world's view?

8. If the Living God, King of the Universe, says you're acceptable, does anyone else, including you, have the right to say you're unacceptable?

9. Is God's love enough to satisfy you even if you're not the person you want to be?

10. What can you thank God for in this situation?

Note: If you're feeling inadequate because of sin, then God wants you to address your sin and work on being transformed through the renewing of your mind (Hebrews 12, Romans 12:1-2). But He's a loving God who wants to help you, not a condemning God who wants to beat you up (Hosea, Romans 8:1, Revelations 12:10).

Possible things you'll need to accept: that you'll never be as good as you want to be, that you can't hide your faults and sins from others, and that you can't live life without messing up at times. Fortunately, everyone else in the world is in the same boat, and God is enough to make up for our shortcomings!

Possible things you'll need to confess: caring more about becoming a perfect person than about loving God and others well, caring more about getting others to love and accept you than about getting yourself to love and accept others, and spending so much time trying to be acceptable in the world's eyes that you don't have time to spend with God.

Bible Verses

Psalm 139:13-15 For You formed my inward parts; You wove me in my mother's womb. I will give thanks to You, for I am fearfully and wonderfully made; Wonderful are Your works, and my soul knows it very well. My frame was not hidden from You when I was made in secret, and skillfully wrought in the depths of the earth.

Isaiah 62:4a, 5b It will no longer be said to you, "Forsaken," Nor to your land will it any longer be said, "Desolate"; But you will be called, "My delight is in her," And your land, "Married"; for the Lord delights in you, and as the bridegroom rejoices over the bride, so your God will rejoice over you.

Jeremiah 31:20 "Is Ephraim My dear son? Is he a delightful child? Indeed, as often as I have spoken against him, I certainly still remember him; Therefore My heart yearns for him; I will surely have mercy on him," declares the Lord.

Jeremiah 31:3-4 The Lord appeared to him from afar, saying, "I have loved you with an everlasting love; therefore I have drawn you with lovingkindness. Again I will build you and you will be rebuilt, O virgin of Israel! Again you will take up your tambourines, and go forth to the dances of the merrymakers."

Zephaniah 3:17 The Lord your God is in your midst, a victorious warrior. He will exult over you with joy, He will be quiet in His love, He will rejoice over you with shouts of joy.

Ephesians 2:10 For we are His workmanship, created in Christ Jesus for good works, which God prepared beforehand so that we would walk in them.

Romans 5:8 But God demonstrates His own love toward us, in that while we were yet sinners, Christ died for us.

1 Peter 2:9 But you are a chosen race, a royal priesthood, a holy nation, a people for God's own possession, so that you may proclaim the excellencies of Him who has called you out of darkness into His marvelous light.

1 Samuel 16:7 But the Lord said to Samuel, "Do not look at his appearance or at the height of his stature, because I have rejected him; for God sees not as man sees, for man looks at the outward appearance, but the Lord looks at the heart."

See also: discontentment, regret, worry, and other insecurity questions and Bible verses.

Insecurity: Feeling Rejected or Condemned

Note: Depending on why you're feeling rejected or condemned, the people pleasing questions might be more helpful.

1. Is it possible to live life without ever being rejected or condemned? (If not, what's the sad truth you'll have to accept right from the beginning?)

2. What did this person do to make you feel rejected or condemned? Be specific.

3. Are you sure this person is rejecting or condemning you? If not, what else might explain their behavior?

4. Does this person do that sort of thing with other people, or does he only do it with you? (If he only does it with you, why do you think he only does it with you?)

5. Do you think his behavior is a sign that he doesn't love or respect you in particular, or is this just an example of the way he responds to people in general?

6. Did you do anything to make this person reject you or condemn you? If so, what did you do? (If not, skip to #8)

7. Do you think God wanted you to do that? Explain.

   a. **Yes:** If so, are you willing to be rejected and condemned for God?

   b. **No:** If not, what do you think God wants you to do now, given the fact that you can't change what's already been done? (For example: apologize, make restitution, let it go, try to change, etc.)

   c. **Not sure:** Was your action loving? If not, was there a good reason for doing it, keeping 1 Corinthians 13 in mind?

   d. **God doesn't care:** Would you rather have this person like you and accept you, or would you rather keep doing what you're doing? (Remember, you can't control the other person.)

8. Is there anything you need to accept about this person and the way he handles relationships? *

9. Is God's love enough to satisfy you even if this person rejects or condemns you?

10. What do you think God wants to do for you in the midst of this difficult situation? (See insecurity verses and Hebrews 12:11 for ideas.)

11. Who are you in God's eyes and how does He feel about you? (Spend some time on this one.)

12. How do you think God wants you to respond to this person who is condemning or rejecting you? *

13. Is there anything you need to accept?

14. What can you thank God for in this situation?

* Note: If this person is treating you with disrespect, you may need to put up some boundaries. If this person is abusive, please get professional help as soon as possible.

Possible things you'll need to accept: that people won't always love and respect you the way you want to be loved and respected, that you're not always easy to love and respect (none of us are), and that no one except God is capable of loving and accepting you perfectly. Also, remember that just because someone disagrees with what you're doing, that doesn't mean they don't love and respect you. Usually, it just means they disagree with what you're doing.

Possible things you'll need to confess: any sins you committed that made this person reject or condemn you, rejecting or condemning them in retaliation, focusing more on getting others to love and respect you rather than getting yourself to love and respect others, and caring too much about what others think.

Bible Verses

Psalm 3:3 But You, O Lord, are a shield about me, my glory, and the One who lifts my head.

Psalm 27:1, 3-5 The Lord is my light and my salvation; whom shall I fear? The Lord is the defense of my life; whom shall I dread? Though a host encamp against me, my heart will not fear; though war arise against me, in spite of this I shall be confident. One thing I have asked from the Lord, that I shall seek: that I may dwell in the house of the Lord all the days of my life, to behold the beauty of the Lord and to meditate in His temple. For in the day of trouble He will conceal me in His tabernacle; in the secret place of His tent He will hide me; He will lift me up on a rock.

Ecclesiastes 7:21-22 Also, do not take seriously all words which are spoken, so that you will not hear your servant cursing you. For you also have realized that you likewise have many times cursed others.

1 Samuel 30:6 Moreover David was greatly distressed because the people spoke of stoning him, for all the people were embittered, each one because of his sons and his daughters. But David strengthened himself in the Lord his God.

Romans 8:31 What then shall we say to these things? If God is for us, who is against us?

See also: discontentment, fear of condemnation (starting a habit), judgment, worry, and other insecurity questions.

Insecurity: People Pleasing

1. Why do you want to make this person happy? (Or what is this person expecting you to do?)

2. What will make him happy?

3. Are you able to make that happen? (If not, what will you need to accept?)

4. Will that really make him happy? Explain.

5. Are you:

   a. Tempted to do something God doesn't want you to do (or not do something God wants you to do) just so you can make this person happy? Explain.

   b. Interfering with what God wants to do in this person's life by always trying to make him happy? Explain.

   c. Remembering that only God can fill this person up and make him happy?

   d. Neglecting your responsibilities (as a parent, for example) just to avoid making this person mad?

   e. Caring too much about what this person thinks?

6. How would you handle this situation if you didn't have to worry about disappointing this person? Why would you handle it that way?

7. How do you think God wants you to handle this situation?

8. Why do you think He wants you to handle it that way?

9. What would you need to give up or risk to do what God wants you to do?

10. Is there anything you need to accept?

11. What can you thank God for in this situation?

Note: If you're having a hard time making a decision, look at the starting a habit/decision questions.

Possible things you'll need to accept: that you can't make everyone happy no matter how hard you try, that sometimes people are unhappy and there's nothing you can do about it, that some people will get mad at you if you tell them no, and that sometimes you need to tell them no. It's also good to remember that just because people are unhappy, it doesn't mean they don't love you. More often than not, it just means they're unhappy.

Possible things you'll need to confess: basing your decisions on what others want you to do rather than on what God wants you to do, neglecting your responsibilities in order to make everyone happy, focusing more on getting others to love and respect you rather than getting yourself to love and respect others, and making an idol of avoiding conflict or getting everyone to like you.

Bible Verses

Proverbs 29:25 The fear of man brings a snare, but he who trusts in the Lord will be exalted.

2 Corinthians 5:9 Therefore we also have as our ambition, whether at home or absent, to be pleasing to Him.

Galatians 1:10 For am I now seeking the favor of men, or of God? Or am I striving to please men? If I were still trying to please men, I would not be a bond-servant of Christ.

Colossians 3:23-24 Whatever you do, do your work heartily, as for the Lord rather than for men, knowing that from the Lord you will receive the reward of the inheritance. It is the Lord Christ whom you serve.

1 Thessalonians 2:4 But just as we have been approved by God to be entrusted with the gospel, so we speak, not as pleasing men, but God who examines our hearts.

1 Peter 1:22 Since you have in obedience to the truth purified your souls for a sincere love of the brethren, fervently love one another from the heart.

See also: anger, fear of condemnation (starting a habit), decisions, discontentment, frustration, greed/lust, worry, and other insecurity questions and Bible verses.

Insecurity: Self-Condemnation

1. Why do you think you're a failure (terrible person, bad Christian, loser, etc.)?

2. Does that really make you a failure (terrible person/bad Christian, etc.)? Why or why not? *

3. Whose standards are you using to determine whether or not you're acceptable?

4. What does God think of those standards?

5. Who are you in God's eyes, and how does He feel about you? (See insecurity/feeling inadequate Bible verses for ideas.)

6. God is not a condemning perfectionist (see verses below). He's a loving Father who says, "Come to me, my beloved, and let me help." In what areas do you need help?

7. Take some time to ask Him to help you with those areas.

8. Is there anything you need to accept?

9. Is there anything God wants you to do?

10. What can you thank God for in this situation?

* If you're having a hard time answering this question, look through the insecurity verses and think about grace. If you're going the bad Christian route, think about the life of David and Romans 3:23.

Possible things you'll need to accept: that you'll never be as good as you want to be, that others will see your imperfections (just as you see their imperfections), and that you'll fail at times. Everyone does—it's part of the human condition, so you might as well get used to it!

Possible things you'll need to confess: condemning someone God loves (you!), giving yourself permission to give up because you feel like a failure, and making "success" more important than God wants you to make it.

Bible Verses

Psalm 37:23-24 The steps of a man are established by the Lord, and He delights in his way. When he falls, he will not be hurled headlong, because the Lord is the One who holds his hand.

Psalm 145:8, 14 The Lord is gracious and merciful; slow to anger and great in lovingkindness. The Lord sustains all who fall and raises up all who are bowed down.

Psalm 147:2-3 The Lord builds up Jerusalem; He gathers the outcasts of Israel. He heals the brokenhearted and binds up their wounds.

Isaiah 30:18 Therefore the Lord longs to be gracious to you, and therefore He waits on high to have compassion on you. For the Lord is a God of justice; how blessed are all those who long for Him.

Isaiah 54:10 "For the mountains may depart and the hills be removed, but my steadfast love shall not depart from you, and my covenant of peace shall not be removed," says the Lord, who has compassion on you.

Jeremiah 31:20 "Is Ephraim My dear son? Is he a delightful child? Indeed, as often as I have spoken against him, I certainly still remember him; Therefore My heart yearns for him; I will surely have mercy on him," declares the Lord.

Romans 7:21, 24-25 I find then the principle that evil is present in me, the one who wants to do good. Wretched man that I am! Who will set me free from the body of this death? Thanks be to God through Jesus Christ our Lord! So then on the one hand I myself with my mind am serving the law of God, but on the other, with my flesh the law of sin.

Romans 8:1-2 Therefore there is now no condemnation for those who are in Christ Jesus. For the law of the Spirit of life in Christ Jesus has set you free from the law of sin and of death.

Romans 8:35, 38-39 Who will separate us from the love of Christ? Will tribulation, or distress, or persecution, or famine, or nakedness, or peril, or sword? For I am convinced that neither death, nor life, nor angels, nor principalities, nor things present, nor things to come, nor powers, nor height, nor depth, nor any other created thing, will be able to separate us from the love of God, which is in Christ Jesus our Lord.

Philippians 1:6 For I am confident of this very thing, that He who began a good work in you will perfect it until the day of Christ Jesus.

Hebrews 4:15-16 For we do not have a high priest who cannot sympathize with our weaknesses, but One who has been tempted in all things as we are, yet without sin. Therefore let us draw near with confidence to the throne of grace, so that we may receive mercy and find grace to help in time of need.

1 John 1:9 If we confess our sins, He is faithful and righteous to forgive us our sins and to cleanse us from all unrighteousness.

See also: the last section in Chapter 6, discontentment, envy, greed/lust, hopelessness (stopping a habit), perfectionism, regret, worry, and other insecurity questions and Bible verses.

Insecurity: Social Situations

1. Why do the people at this gathering intimidate you?

2. If the people at the gathering don't appear to like or respect you, does that automatically mean they don't? What else could it mean?

3. Do you think God wants you to reach out to these people even though you risk rejection? Why or why not? *

4. If so, what attitude does He want you to have? (Philippians 2:4-8)

5. How does God want you to treat the people at this gathering? (1 Corinthians 13:4-8)

6. Is there anything you need to give up or risk to love these people well?

7. Are you in a place of feeling treasured by God so you're able to take that risk? (If not, pray through the feeling inadequate Bible verses.)

8. Is there anything you need to accept?

9. Is there anything you need to trust God with?

10. What can you thank God for in this situation?

* **Note:** There may be situations when the answer to this question is no. The key is to base your actions on what God wants you to do, not on what you feel comfortable doing.

Possible things you'll need to accept: that you can't live life without saying and doing dumb things at times, that not all social situations will be comfortable, that you'll never be as perfect as you want to be, that you'll never be as popular as you want to be, and that if people are going to love and respect you, they'll have to love and respect the imperfect and sometimes unpopular you.

Possible things you'll need to confess: caring more about what others think than what God thinks, caring more about getting others to love you than about getting yourself to love others, doing things God doesn't want you to do in order to be popular, an unwillingness to be uncomfortable and take risks to love others well, and idolatry (making an idol of appearance, popularity, status, comfort, etc.).

See also: discontentment, envy, worry, and other insecurity questions and Bible verses.

Bible Verses

1 Corinthians 13:4-8a Love is patient, love is kind. It does not envy, it does not boast, it is not proud. It does not dishonor others, it is not self-seeking, it is not easily angered, it keeps no record of wrongs. Love does not delight in evil but rejoices with the truth. It always protects, always trusts, always hopes, always perseveres. Love never fails. (NIV)

Philippians 2:4-8 Do not merely look out for your own personal interests, but also for the interests of others. Have this attitude in yourselves which was also in Christ Jesus, who, although He existed in the form of God, did not regard equality with God a thing to be grasped, but emptied Himself, taking the form of a bond-servant and being made in the likeness of men. Being found in appearance as a man, He humbled Himself by becoming obedient to the point of death, even death on a cross.

1 John 3:16 We know love by this, that He laid down His life for us; and we ought to lay down our lives for the brethren.

See also: discontentment, fear of condemnation (starting a habit), worry, and other insecurity questions and Bible verses.

Judgment

1. Is what you're judging a sin or just a different way of doing things?

2. If it's a difference:

   a. Does God want you to make your own standards a law for others to follow?

   b. Are you willing to accept another way of doing things?

3. If it's a sin:

   a. Are you grieving over this person's sin, or are you condemning him for it?

   b. Is your desire to bring this person back to God, or are you more concerned with how his behavior is affecting your life (either directly or indirectly)?

   c. How can you best help this person?

4. How do you compare to the person you're judging? Are you judging from a position of strength or weakness?

   a. **If strength to weakness:**

      - If you've never struggled with this weakness: Do you realize how blessed you are to never have struggled with it?

      - If you've overcome this weakness: Are you thanking God for giving you the strength and desire to overcome it, or are you beginning to believe that it was all your own doing?

   b. **If weakness to weakness:**

      - Why are you condemning it in someone else when you know how hard it is to overcome?

   c. **If weakness to strength:**

- Does this strong person deserve your judgment just because you're weak in this area?

5. Is this person's sin or fault worse than your own sin of condemning him?

6. How do you think God wants you to respond to this person?

7. Is there anything you need to accept?

8. Is there anything you need to confess?

9. What can you thank God for in this situation?

Possible things you'll need to accept: that people do wrong things, that sometimes they get away with the wrong things they do, that your way isn't always the best way or the only way, and that you're not in control.

Possible things you'll need to confess: acting like God when you're not God, turning your own standards into a law for others to follow, caring too much about things God doesn't care about (such as appearance and status), arrogance, pride, and resentment.

Bible Verses

Matthew 7:3-5 Why do you look at the speck that is in your brother's eye, but do not notice the log that is in your own eye? Or how can you say to your brother, 'Let me take the speck out of your eye,' and behold, the log is in your own eye? You hypocrite, first take the log out of your own eye, and then you will see clearly to take the speck out of your brother's eye.

John 3:17 For God did not send the Son into the world to judge the world, but that the world might be saved through Him.

Romans 2:4 Or do you think lightly of the riches of His kindness and tolerance and patience, not knowing that the kindness of God leads you to repentance?

Romans 14:4 Who are you to judge the servant of another? To his own master he stands or falls; and he will stand, for the Lord is able to make him stand.

Romans 14:13 Therefore let us not judge one another anymore, but rather determine this—not to put an obstacle or a stumbling block in a brother's way.

James 4:6 But He gives a greater grace. Therefore it says, "God is opposed to the proud, but gives grace to the humble."

James 4:11-12 Do not speak against one another, brethren. He who speaks against a brother or judges his brother, speaks against the law and judges the law; but if you judge the law, you are not a doer of the law but a judge of it. There is only one Lawgiver and Judge, the One who is able to save and to destroy; but who are you who judge your neighbor?

See also: anger, envy, insecurity, and pride.

Pride

1. Why do you think you're a better person/Christian than this person?

2. Does God think you're better? If not, what does He think?

3. How does putting yourself "above" this person affect your relationship with God and your relationship with this person?

4. Are you remembering that God gave you everything you have, or are you beginning to think it's all your own doing?

5. What has God blessed you with?

6. How does He want you to use those blessings?

7. Is there anything you need to confess?

8. What can you be thankful for in this situation?

Possible things you'll need to accept: that you're not as great as you think you are, that you're not better than others, and that God has given you everything you have.

Possible things you'll need to confess: making more of yourself than you have a right to make, an unwillingness to change, an unwillingness to look at your own sin, an unwillingness to serve others, and a failure to recognize that God is the one who is responsible for your strengths, not you.

Bible Verses

Exodus 3:5 Then He said, "Do not come near here; remove your sandals from your feet, for the place on which you are standing is holy ground."

Deuteronomy 8:17-18a You may say to yourself, "My power and the strength of my hands have produced this wealth for me." But remember the Lord your God, for it is He who gives you the ability to produce wealth. (NIV)

Psalm 138:6 Though the Lord is high, he looks upon the lowly, but the proud he knows from afar. (NIV)

Jeremiah 9:23-24 Thus says the Lord, "Let not a wise man boast of his wisdom, and let not the mighty man boast of his might, let not a rich man boast of his riches; but let him who boasts boast of this, that he understands and knows Me, that I am the Lord who exercises lovingkindness, justice and righteousness on earth; for I delight in these things," declares the Lord.

John 3:30 He must increase, but I must decrease.

1 Corinthians 4:7 For who regards you as superior? What do you have that you did not receive? And if you did receive it, why do you boast as if you had not received it?

2 Corinthians 3:5 Not that we are adequate in ourselves to consider anything as coming from ourselves, but our adequacy is from God.

1 Peter 5:5b Clothe yourselves with humility toward one another, for God is opposed to the proud, but gives grace to the humble.

1 Peter 5:6 Therefore humble yourselves under the mighty hand of God, that He may exalt you at the proper time.

See also: anger, envy, and judgment.

Regret

1. What do you wish you would have done or not done?

2. Do you think God wishes you had done things differently? Why or why not?

3. Since you can't go back and change what you did or didn't do, how do you think God wants you to respond now?

4. How would Satan like you to respond?

5. What can you gain from this experience if you respond the way God wants you to respond?

6. Can God redeem this situation even if you really messed up? Explain.

7. Is there anything you need to accept?

8. Is there anything you need to confess?

9. Do you need to apologize to anyone or make restitution?

10. What can you thank God for in this situation?

Possible things you'll need to accept: that you can't go back and change what you did or didn't do, that your actions sometimes hurt others, that you can't fix everything in life, that you may need to live with the consequences of your actions, and that sometimes you'll make bad choices in life—everyone does. Just remember, God can redeem anything.

Possible things you'll need to confess: not doing something God wanted you to do, doing something God didn't want you to do, and making something more important than God wants you to make it.

Bible Verses

Proverbs 3:5-6 Trust in the Lord with all your heart and do not lean on your own understanding. In all your ways acknowledge Him, and He will make your paths straight.

Jeremiah 29:11 "For I know the plans I have for you," declares the Lord, "plans for welfare and not for calamity to give you a future and a hope."

Philippians 3:13-14 Brethren, I do not regard myself as having laid hold of it yet; but one thing I do: forgetting what lies behind and reaching forward to what lies ahead, I press on toward the goal for the prize of the upward call of God in Christ Jesus.

Romans 8:28 And we know that God causes all things to work together for good to those who love God, to those who are called according to His purpose.

Romans 8:1-2 Therefore there is now no condemnation for those who are in Christ Jesus. For the law of the Spirit of life in Christ Jesus has set you free from the law of sin and of death.

Philippians 4:11b-13 I have learned to be content whatever the circumstances. I know what it is to be in need, and I know what it is to have plenty. I have learned the secret of being content in any and every situation, whether well fed or hungry, whether living in plenty or in want. I can do all things through Him who strengthens me.

1 Thessalonians 5:18 In everything give thanks; for this is God's will for you in Christ Jesus.

1 John 1:9 If we confess our sins, He is faithful and righteous to forgive us our sins and to cleanse us from all unrighteousness.

See also: anger, discontentment, envy, perfectionism, and worry.

Stress: Beginning of Workday

1. Why are you so stressed today?

2. Can you make a list of all the things you need to get done? If so, go ahead and do that.

3. Are you able to accomplish everything on your list today?

   a. **Yes:** If so, why are you feeling so stressed? Consider doing a different set of questions depending on your answer to this question.

   b. **No:** Is there anything you need to accept?

4. Of all the things on your list:

   a. What two things are you dreading the most? Why are you dreading them?

   b. What two things are the most important?

   c. Is there anything you absolutely need to get done today?

   d. Is there anything God wants you to do today that's not even on your list?

5. Looking back over your answers to the last question, make a prioritized, realistic list for the day. If you have problems following the list, turn to the starting a habit questions.

6. How can you love God and others best as you work on your list today?

7. If life is about loving God and others, will it be the end of the world if you don't finish your list today?

Possible things you'll need to accept: that you might not be able to get everything done, that you might not have time to do it as well as you want to do it, and that sometimes life is busy and there's nothing you can do about it.

Possible things you'll need to confess: making recreation, work, projects, or hobbies more important than God wants you to make them, being so busy you don't have time for God, and hurting others in your quest to get things done.

Bible Verses

Psalm 18:29, 34 For by You I can run upon a troop; and by my God I can leap over a wall. He trains my hands for battle so that my arms can bend a bow of bronze.

Psalm 59:16-17 But as for me, I shall sing of Your strength; yes, I shall joyfully sing of Your lovingkindness in the morning, for You have been my stronghold and a refuge in the day of my distress. O my strength, I will sing praises to You; for God is my stronghold, the God who shows me lovingkindness.

Isaiah 40:31 Yet those who wait for the Lord will gain new strength; they will mount up with wings like eagles, they will run and not get tired, they will walk and not become weary.

Jeremiah 42:6b Whether it is pleasant or unpleasant, we will listen to the voice of the Lord our God.

Lamentations 3:22-23 The Lord's lovingkindnesses indeed never cease, for his compassions never fail. They are new every morning; great is Your faithfulness.

Luke 10:41-42 But the Lord answered and said to her, "Martha, Martha, you are worried and bothered about so many things; but only one thing is necessary, for Mary has chosen the good part, which shall not be taken away from her."

2 Corinthians 12:9 And He has said to me, "My grace is sufficient for you, for power is perfected in weakness." Most gladly, therefore, I will rather boast about my weaknesses, so that the power of Christ may dwell in me.

Philippians 4:13 I can do all things through Him who strengthens me.

See also: dread, lack of confidence, procrastination, perfectionism, and worry.

Stress: General and End of Workday

Why are you so stressed right now? Be specific. Renew your mind, using the list below as a guide.

If you're stressed because…

1. **You feel like you have too much to do:** see beginning of workday stress, lack of time, or the questions below.

2. **You feel like you have to be perfect:** see perfectionism or reward/ obsession.

3. **You're frustrated that life is so hard:** see frustration or tired of the struggle/breaking a habit questions.

4. **You're worried, annoyed, or insecure:** see worry, anger, or insecurity.

5. **You're worried about what people will think if you don't perform well:** see people pleasing, worry, or fear of condemnation.

6. **You said or did something dumb today:** see regret.

7. **You didn't get enough done today:** see regret, self-condemnation, reward/obsession, or questions below.

8. **You can't stop thinking about all you have to do:** see self-condemnation, greed/lust, worry, reward/obsession, or the questions below.

9. **You don't want to do anything else after such a long day:** see discontentment.

10. **You don't think you should *have* to do anything else after such a long day:** see entitlement.

Possible things you'll need to accept: that life is busy sometimes, that you're not perfect, that you're not in control, that you can't accomplish as much as you'd like to accomplish, that sometimes you'll look back on your day and think, *I didn't get even one thing done*, and that sometimes you won't get everything done even if you work hard all day.

Possible things you'll need to confess: making an idol of your to-do list, work, hobbies, recreation, and/or free time, being so consumed by your to-do list that you don't have time for God and others, making life about things other than God, and hurting others in your quest to get things done.

Overwhelmed with Work

1. What do you want to accomplish, and when do you want to accomplish it by?

2. Is that possible? Why or why not?

   a. **Yes:** If so, do you think God wants you to work on that? Why or why not? (If you don't think He wants you to work on it, go on to #2b. If you do think He wants you to work on it, go to #6.)

   b. **No:** If not, what would be the next best option?

      1. **Quit.** If you can't do it on your terms, don't do anything.

      2. **Stress.** Keep demanding the impossible even though it's driving you (and possibly others) crazy.

      3. **Hire it out.** Hire someone to do the work so you can finish it on time.

      4. **Lower your standards.** Keep the current target date but lower your standards and expectations so you can finish it on time without stress.

      5. **Change the target date.** Keep your high standards, but change the target date so you have a goal you can actually accomplish.

3. What would be the best thing to do, and why do you think that's best?

4. What will you have to sacrifice or accept if you choose that option?

5. What will you gain if you choose that option?

6. Are there any activities you need to let go of so you have more time to work on this goal? Explain.

7. Is there anything you need to trust God with?

8. What can you thank God for in this situation?

Bible Verses

Psalm 63:6-8 When I remember You on my bed, I meditate on You in the night watches, for You have been my help, and in the shadow of Your wings I sing for joy. My soul clings to You; Your right hand upholds me.

Isaiah 26:3 The steadfast of mind You will keep in perfect peace, because he trusts in you.

Matthew 11:28-30 Come to Me, all who are weary and heavy-laden, and I will give you rest. Take My yoke upon you and learn from Me, for I am gentle and humble in heart, and you will find rest for your souls. For My yoke is easy and My burden is light.

Luke 10:41-42 But the Lord answered and said to her, "Martha, Martha, you are worried and bothered about so many things; but only one thing is necessary, for Mary has chosen the good part, which shall not be taken away from her."

John 14:27 Peace I leave with you; My peace I give to you; not as the world gives do I give to you. Do not let your heart be troubled, nor let it be fearful.

John 15:4-5 Abide in Me, and I in you. As the branch cannot bear fruit of itself unless it abides in the vine, so neither can you unless you abide in Me. I am the vine, you are the branches; he who abides in Me and I in him, he bears much fruit, for apart from Me you can do nothing.

James 4:13-15 Come now, you who say, "Today or tomorrow we will go to such and such a city, and spend a year there and engage in business and make a profit." Yet you do not know what your life will be like tomorrow. You are just a vapor that appears for a little while and then vanishes away. Instead, you ought to say, "If the Lord wills, we will live and also do this or that."

Worry/Fear

1. What are you worried about? Be specific.

2. What's the worst that can happen?

    a. What are the odds that the worst will happen?

    b. Are you willing to accept the worst if God allows the worst to happen?

3. What's the best that can happen?

    a. Why do you want that to happen?

    b. Do you think God wants that to happen? Why or why not?

4. Are God's priorities different than your priorities in this situation? If so, how are they different?

5. Are you able to control the outcome in this situation? Why or why not?

6. Are you able to influence this situation? If so, what could you do?

7. Do you think God wants you to do that? Why or why not?

8. What do you think God wants to do for you (and/or your loved ones) in this situation? See verses below for ideas.

9. Is there anything you need to trust God with?

10. Is God worthy of your trust? Why or why not?

11. How can you love God and others best in this situation?

12. Is there anything you need to accept?

13. What can you thank God for in this situation?

Note: If you're having a hard time thinking of things to be thankful for, try meditating on the attributes of God. Thank Him for who He is (all-knowing, all-powerful, all-loving, just, merciful, compassionate, etc.) and why that makes a difference in this situation.

Possible things you'll need to accept: that the unthinkable will happen, that you're not in control, that there's often nothing you can do to prevent bad things from happening, and that you might not get what you want.

Possible things you'll need to confess: making things more important than God wants you to make them, not holding people and things with open hands, trying to control things God doesn't want you to control, and a lack of trust in God.

Bible Verses

Psalm 61:1-2 Hear my cry, O God; give heed to my prayer. From the end of the earth I call to You when my heart is faint; lead me to the rock that is higher than I.

Psalm 91:1 He who dwells in the shelter of the Most High will abide in the shadow of the Almighty. I will say to the Lord, "My refuge and my fortress, my God, in whom I trust!" For it is He who delivers you from the snare of the trapper and from the deadly pestilence. He will cover you with His pinions, and under His wings you may seek refuge; His faithfulness is a shield and bulwark.

Proverbs 3:5-6 Trust in the Lord with all your heart and do not lean on your own understanding. In all your ways acknowledge Him, and He will make your paths straight.

Isaiah 26:3-4 The steadfast of mind You will keep in perfect peace, because he trusts in you. Trust in the Lord forever, for in God the Lord, we have an everlasting Rock.

Isaiah 41:10 Do not fear, for I am with you; do not anxiously look about you, for I am your God. I will strengthen you, surely I will help you, surely I will uphold you with My righteous right hand.

Jeremiah 32:27 Behold, I am the Lord, the God of all flesh; is anything too difficult for Me?

Jeremiah 32:17 Ah Lord God! Behold, You have made the heavens and the earth by Your great power and by your outstretched arm! Nothing is too difficult for you.

Matthew 6:27, 33-34 And who of you by being worried can add a single hour to his life? But seek first His kingdom and His righteousness, and all these things will be added to you. So do not worry about tomorrow; for tomorrow will care for itself. Each day has enough trouble of its own.

Matthew 19:26 And looking at them Jesus said to them, "With people this is impossible, but with God all things are possible."

Luke 19:10 For the Son of Man has come to seek and to save that which was lost.

Romans 5:3-5 And not only this, but we also exult in our tribulations, knowing that tribulation brings about perseverance; and perseverance, proven character; and proven character, hope; and hope does not disappoint, because the love of God has been poured out within our hearts through the Holy Spirit who was given to us.

Romans 8:26-28 In the same way the Spirit also helps our weakness; for we do not know how to pray as we should, but the Spirit Himself intercedes for us with groanings too deep for words; and He who searches the hearts knows what the mind of the Spirit is, because He intercedes for the saints according to the will of God. And we know that God causes all things to work together for good to those who love God, to those who are called according to His purpose.

Philippians 4:6-7 Be anxious for nothing, but in everything by prayer and supplication with thanksgiving let your requests be made known to God. And the peace of God, which surpasses all comprehension, will guard your hearts and your minds in Christ Jesus.

2 Timothy 1:7 For God has not given us a spirit of timidity, but of power and love and discipline.

1 John 4:4b Greater is He who is within you than he who is in the world.

See also: anger, discontentment, greed/lust, judgment, and insecurity.

STOPPING A
HABIT
OR
BREAKING FREE
FROM A SIN

> QUESTIONS
> AND
> BIBLE VERSES

Boredom

Note: If you're bored because you don't know what to do, try the beginning of the day stress questions or the questions below. If you're bored because you know what to do and don't want to do it, try the procrastination, discontentment, or dread questions. If you're bored in an "I can't stand life" sort of way, try the discontentment, greed/lust, or boredom/starting a habit questions.

1. What is your next scheduled activity?

2. How much time do you need to fill until your scheduled activity?

3. Is your habit a good way to fill this time? Why or why not?

4. What are some other things you could do with this block of time? List a few ideas.

5. What would be the best use of your time right now?

6. What would you gain by using your time this way?

7. Is there anything you need to accept?

Bible Verses

Ephesians 5:15-16 Therefore be careful how you walk, not as unwise men but as wise, making the most of your time, because the days are evil.

Philippians 4:11-13 Not that I speak from want, for I have learned to be content in whatever circumstances I am. I know how to get along with humble means, and I also know how to live in prosperity; in any and every circumstance I have learned the secret of being filled and going hungry, both of having abundance and suffering need. I can do all things through Him who strengthens me.

Philippians 4:19 And my God will supply all your needs according to His riches in glory in Christ Jesus.

1 Thessalonians 5:18 In everything give thanks; for this is God's will for you in Christ Jesus.

1 John 3:16 We know love by this, that He laid down His life for us; and we ought to lay down our lives for the brethren.

Tips

The easiest way to eliminate boredom habiting is to get an exciting life. Unfortunately, this isn't always possible, nor is it always what God wants! There are all kinds of exciting things we could do that God wouldn't approve of.

If you struggle with boredom, spend some time talking to God about it. How do you think He wants you to spend your time? If you're already doing what God wants you to do, try to change your view of excitement.

My friend Tanya helped me with this one day when I was complaining about my boring life. She said, "Barb, what does excitement look like from a spiritual perspective?" I thought for a moment and reluctantly answered, "Well, I suppose from a spiritual perspective, excitement would be growing closer to God and helping others grow closer to Him."

She had me. My life was exciting from a spiritual perspective. I just wasn't seeing it through biblical eyes. The interesting thing is that we can all have exciting lives from a biblical perspective no matter how dull they are from a cultural perspective. We just need to change the way we look at life.

Carelessness

1. Why do you feel like it's not a big deal if you break your boundaries?

2. If you break your boundaries right now, will you be more inclined to break them later? Why or why not?

3. How does the practice of your habit affect the following?

    a. Your relationship with God

    b. Your relationship with others

    c. Your job and/or ministry

    d. Your health

    e. Your personal well being

4. If you want to break this habit, will you eventually have to make the sacrifice to follow your boundaries all the time, even when it's hard to follow them?

5. When do you most need boundaries?

Bible Verses

Romans 13:14 But put on the Lord Jesus Christ, and make no provision for the flesh in regard to its lusts.

1 Corinthians 6:12 All things are lawful for me, but not all things are profitable. All things are lawful for me, but I will not be mastered by anything.

1 Timothy 4:7b Discipline yourself for the purpose of godliness.

1 Thessalonians 5:6 So then let us not sleep as others do, but let us be alert and sober.

1 Peter 5:8 Be of sober spirit, be on the alert. Your adversary, the devil, prowls around like a roaring lion, seeking someone to devour.

Tips

One of the hardest habits to break is a non-sin habit that's acceptable in the culture: habits like Facebook, checking emails, and texting. Because the habit is so acceptable, we tend to think, *Is it really that big of a deal if I break my boundaries?* Here's the truth: If it weren't a big deal, you wouldn't be doing these questions. You're trying to break your habit because it's messing up your life in some way. The secret to breaking your habit is to keep reminding yourself of *how* it's messing up your life. The carelessness questions should help with that.

If you already know you need boundaries—but just keep forgetting them—try putting sticky notes all over your house and/or workplace to remind yourself to follow your boundaries. You'll probably only need to leave them up the first week or two, but it will help you get started.

Despair

1. What's going on in your life today that's making you feel so desperate? Be specific.

2. If life is about "living the good life," is this a terrible situation? Why or why not?

3. If life is about loving God and others, is this a terrible situation? Why or why not?

4. How does God feel about you (or the ones you love) in the midst of this difficult situation? (See insecurity/feeling inadequate verses for ideas.)

5. What would He like to do for you (or the ones you love) in this difficult situation? (See verses below and Romans 5:3-5.)

6. How do you think He wants you to handle this crisis?

7. What will you (or your loved ones) gain if you do what He wants you to do?

8. What do you think God wants to teach you (or your loved ones) through this trial?

9. What can you thank Him for?

Bible Verses

Psalm 27:13 I would have despaired unless I had believed that I would see the goodness of the Lord in the land of the living.

Psalm 61:1-4 Hear my cry, O God; give heed to my prayer. From the end of the earth I call to You when my heart is faint; lead me to the rock that is higher than I. For You have been a refuge for me, a tower of strength against the enemy. Let me dwell in your tent forever; let me take refuge in the shelter of Your wings.

Psalm 63:1 O God, You are my God; I shall seek You earnestly; my soul thirsts for You, my flesh yearns for You, in a dry and weary land where there is so water.

Psalm 40:1-3a I waited patiently for the LORD; he turned to me and heard my cry. He lifted me out of the slimy pit, out of the mud and mire; he set my feet on a rock and gave me a firm place to stand. He put a new song in my mouth, a hymn of praise to our God.

Jeremiah 29:11 "For I know the plans I have for you," declares the Lord, "plans for welfare and not for calamity to give you a future and a hope."

Romans 5:3-5 And not only this, but we also exult in our tribulations, knowing that tribulation brings about perseverance; and perseverance, proven character; and proven character, hope; and hope does not disappoint, because the love of God has been poured out within our hearts through the Holy Spirit who was given to us.

2 Corinthians 4:8-10 We are afflicted in every way, but not crushed; perplexed, but not despairing; persecuted, but not forsaken; struck down, but not destroyed; always carrying about in the body the dying of Jesus, so that the life of Jesus also may be manifested in our body.

Tips

With emotional habiting, we turn to our habits to cope with life. Despair habiting is like emotional habiting on steroids. It's for those days when your whole world feels like it's falling apart. Those are the days when it's hardest to go to God for help because we're in such emotional turmoil.

I often find that truth journaling, listening to praise music, or praying with thanksgiving (Philippians 4:6-7) works best in those situations, but I sometimes use these despair questions. If you try these questions and they don't help, ask yourself, "What other emotion am I feeling?"

Then go to the questions and Bible verses for that emotion and have another conversation with God. Try to keep visiting with Him until you're at peace. If you can't reach that point, know that another day is coming and often we have a good day after we have a bad day.

Also, please consider seeing a counselor if this is an ongoing struggle. Sometimes it helps to have a listening ear and you may need a listening ear who has been trained to help you with your struggles.

Emotional Habiting

1. What's going on in your life that makes you want to break your boundaries?

2. What emotion are you experiencing?

3. Will breaking your boundaries make you feel better? If so, for how long?

4. Will it solve your problems?

5. Will it create any new problems or make the situation worse in some way? Explain.

6. How do you think God wants you to handle this situation?

7. What do your boundaries protect you from?

8. Do you need that protection today?

9. What do you think God wants to teach you through this trial?

10. Is there anything you need to accept?

11. What can you thank God for in this situation?

Bible Verses

Psalm 31:1-3, 7 In You, O Lord, I have taken refuge; let me never be ashamed; in Your righteousness deliver me. Incline Your ear to me, rescue me quickly; be to me a rock of strength, a stronghold to save me. For you are my rock and my fortress; for Your name's sake You will lead me and guide me. I will rejoice and be glad in Your lovingkindness, because You have seen my affliction; You have known the troubles of my soul.

Psalm 37:39 But the salvation of the righteous is from the Lord; He is their strength in time of trouble.

Psalm 138:3 On the day I called, You answered me; You made me bold with strength in my soul.

Philippians 4:6-7 Be anxious for nothing, but in everything by prayer and supplication with thanksgiving let your requests be made known to God. And the peace of God, which surpasses all comprehension, will guard your hearts and your minds in Christ Jesus.

Philippians 4:19 And my God will supply all your needs according to His riches in glory in Christ Jesus.

Tips

The telltale sign of emotional habiting is that you feel driven to do your habit. You're not thinking, *Oh, that would nice to do my habit*; You're thinking, *I need my habit!!*

Emotional habiting is triggered by something else going on in your life, usually something bad. The best way to break free from it is to get rid of the emotions that are driving your behavior. Ask yourself, "What emotion am I experiencing?" Then go through the questions and Bible verses for that emotion.

What usually happens when you take the time to work through the emotion is that your desire to do your habit will disappear. If you don't take the time, that emotion has to go somewhere. Often, it goes out looking for your habit.

Entitlement

1. Why do you feel like you deserve your habit in this particular situation?

2. Do you think God agrees with your outlook on life? Why or why not?

3. What usually happens when you live by your rights and feelings in this area of your life?

4. Would your life be better if you gave up your rights and held life and your habit with open hands? Why or why not?

5. Are boundaries easy to follow or do you usually have to give up something to follow them?

6. What will you have to give up to follow your boundaries this time?

7. What will your life look like a few months down the road if you develop the habit of consistently following your boundaries?

8. When you think of all you'll gain, is it worth the sacrifice?

Bible Verses

Jeremiah 2:13 For My people have committed two evils: they have forsaken Me, the fountain of living waters, to hew for themselves cisterns, broken cisterns that can hold no water.

Romans 13:14 But put on the Lord Jesus Christ, and make no provision for the flesh in regard to its lusts.

Galatians 5:13 For you were called to freedom, brethren; only do not turn your freedom into an opportunity for the flesh, but through love serve one another.

Philippians 3:7-8 But whatever things were gain to me, those things I have counted as loss for the sake of Christ. More than that, I count all things to be loss in view of the surpassing value of knowing Christ Jesus my Lord, for whom I have suffered the loss of all things, and count them but rubbish so that I may gain Christ.

Philippians 3:18-19 For many walk, of whom I often told you, and now tell you even weeping, that they are enemies of the cross of Christ, whose end is destruction, whose god is their appetite, and whose glory is in their shame, who set their minds on earthly things.

James 4:6b God is opposed to the proud, but gives grace to the humble.

1 Peter 1:14-16 As obedient children, do not be conformed to the former lusts which were yours in your ignorance, but like the Holy One who called you, be holy yourselves also in all your behavior, because it is written, "You shall be holy, for I am holy."

1 John 2:15-16 Do not love the world not the things in the world. If anyone loves the world, the love of the Father is not in him. For all that is in the world, the lust of the flesh and the lust of the eyes and the boastful pride of life, is not from the Father, but is from the world.

Tips

It's hard to break free from our habits because we hear the message everywhere we go: *Life should be fair. You shouldn't have to suffer. You deserve the good life!* So when something bad or unfair is going on in our lives, we automatically reach for our habits.

The best way to break free from entitlement habiting is to adopt a biblical perspective of life. God never said, "You deserve the good life." Instead, He said, "If you want to follow me, you have to give up everything" (Matthew 19:16-22, Matthew 16:21-28).

When we hold our habits with tightly clenched fists, we're basically saying, "I deserve this, God, and I'm not willing to give it up!"

God replies, "Your habit will never make you happy. Come to me and I'll give you the abundant life."

The more we hold our habits with open hands, willing to give up all things for God, the more content we'll be. If you want to gain victory over entitlement habiting, learn to hold your habit—and your "right to the good life"—with open hands.

Failure

1. Are you one of those rare (and possibly non-existent) people who can follow your boundaries effortlessly and perfectly without ever breaking them? If not, what's the sad truth you'll have to accept right from the beginning?

2. Since you can't change the past, what do you think God wants you to do now?

   a. Forget about the boundaries the rest of the day and start fresh in the morning.

   b. Beat yourself up and tell yourself what a loser you are.

   c. Remember that you're in a spiritual battle. Continue to fight the battle with spiritual weapons, knowing that you'll fail at times. Be extra diligent with your weapons in the next 24 hours so you don't break your boundaries again.

3. Why do you think God wants you to take that option?

4. How does it make you feel to know that God understands what you're going through? (Hebrews 4:15-16)

5. Do you think you can break free from this habit without making your boundaries absolute boundaries? Why or why not?

6. What will your life look like when you're free from the control of this habit?

7. When you think of what you'll gain, is it worth the sacrifice to follow your boundaries the rest of the day?

Bible Verses

John 8:10-11 Straightening up, Jesus said to her, "Woman, where are they? Did no one condemn you?" She said, "No one, Lord." And Jesus said, "I do not condemn you, either. Go. From now on sin no more."

Romans 6:1-2 What shall we say then? Are we to continue in sin so that grace may increase? May it never be! How shall we who died to sin still live in it?

Philippians 1:6 For I am confident of this very thing, that He who began a good work in you will perfect it until the day of Christ Jesus.

Philippians 4:13 I can do all things through Him who strengthens me.

Hebrews 4:15-16 For we do not have a high priest who cannot sympathize with our weaknesses, but One who has been tempted in all things as we are, yet without sin. Therefore let us draw near with confidence to the throne of grace, so that we may receive mercy and find grace to help in time of need.

James 1:12 Blessed is the man who perseveres under trial; for once he has been approved, he will receive the crown of life, which the Lord has promised to those who love Him.

Tips

The best way to break free from failure habiting is to renew your mind *every single time* you break your boundaries. The sooner the better. Here's what happens when we don't renew our minds: We either beat ourselves up, or we start breaking our boundaries right and left.

Don't do that! Satan is the condemner of the saints and he'd like nothing better than to see you beat yourself up or spend the rest of your life being controlled by your habit (Revelations 12:10).

God on the other hand wants to help you *break* that habit. And He's the only one who has the power to make it happen. That's why it's so vital to skip the whole beating-yourself-up session and go directly to God for comfort, truth, and moral support (Hebrews 4:15-16). He'll help you identify and take off the lies that are making you want to do your habit and give you the truth that will set you free.

When you renew your mind, try to remember what you were thinking before you broke your boundaries and renew your mind with those thoughts in mind. If you can't remember what you were thinking, use the failure questions and Bible verses.

Hopelessness

1. How many years have you been struggling with this habit?

2. How many years (or weeks) have you been diligent about applying truth to the lies that are fueling your habit?

3. On a scale of 1 to 10, how diligent have you been?

4. When you think of how long you've been renewing your mind compared to how long you've had this problem, is it realistic to expect 100% victory at this point? Why or why not?

5. Since you can't change the past, what do you think God wants you to do now?

   a. Give up.

   b. Beat yourself up and think about what a loser you are.

   c. Sit back and wait for God to change you in His time.

   d. Remember that you're in a spiritual battle, and expect it to be difficult. Fight the battle with spiritual weapons and renew your mind every time you feel like breaking your boundaries. Trust God to change you in His time.

6. What should you expect if you choose the last option? (Think of Jesus in the desert, Jesus in Gethsemane, Job's attack by Satan, and Hebrews 12:11.)

7. Is there anything you need to accept?

8. Is there anything you need to do?

9. Would it help to have an accountability partner? If so, whom could you ask?

Bible Verses

Psalm 144:1-2a Blessed be the Lord, my rock, who trains my hands for war, and my fingers for battle; my lovingkindness and my fortress, my stronghold and my deliverer, my shield and He in whom I take refuge.

Isaiah 43:18-19 Do not call to mind the former things, or ponder things of the past. Behold, I will do something new, now it will spring forth; will you not be aware of it? I will even make a roadway in the wilderness, rivers in the desert.

Jeremiah 32:27 Behold, I am the Lord, the God of all flesh; is anything too difficult for Me?

Jeremiah 32:17 Ah Lord God! Behold, You have made the heavens and the earth by Your great power and by your outstretched arm! Nothing is too difficult for you.

Romans 12:2 And do not be conformed to this world, but be transformed by the renewing of your mind, so that you may prove what the will of God is, that which is good and acceptable and perfect.

Galatians 6:9 Let us not lose heart in doing good, for in due time we will reap if we do not grow weary.

Philippians 1:6 For I am confident of this very thing, that He who began a good work in you will perfect it until the day of Christ Jesus.

Philippians 3:13-14 Brethren, I do not regard myself as having laid hold of it yet; but one thing I do: forgetting what lies behind and reaching forward to what lies ahead, I press on toward the goal for the prize of the upward call of God in Christ Jesus.

Hebrews 10:36 For you have need of endurance, so that when you have done the will of God, you may receive what was promised.

Hebrews 12:11 All discipline for the moment seems not to be joyful, but sorrowful; yet to those who have been trained by it, afterwards it yields the peaceful fruit of righteousness.

James 1:2-4 Consider it all joy, my brethren, when you encounter various trials, knowing that the testing of your faith produces endurance. And let endurance have its perfect result, that you may be perfect and complete, lacking in nothing.

Tips

Hopelessness is an attitude that says, "I'll never get over this anyway so why bother?" It usually kicks in after a period of failure. The key to overcoming hopeless habiting is to realize that failure isn't the end of the world. It's just another step on a path that is heading toward victory. Use your failure as an opportunity to go to God and learn from your mistakes.

If you renew your mind every time you break your boundaries, you turn your failure into a victory because God will use the truth to transform you. Not as soon as you'd like, but it will happen eventually. Just keep plugging away and have faith that God will work in you.

I'll Start Tomorrow

1. What are your boundaries?

2. Is there ever a good (i.e. easy) time to start following your boundaries? Why or why not?

3. What sacrifices will you have to make to break (or control) this habit?

4. Is it possible to break your habit without making those sacrifices? Why or why not?

5. How does the practice of your habit affect the following:

   a. Your work

   b. Your health and personal well-being

   c. Your relationship with God

   d. Your relationship with others

6. Are you the type of person who can go without boundaries in this area without messing up your life in some way?

7. Do you think God wants you to have boundaries in this area of your life? Why or why not?

8. How would your life change if you were able to break (or control) this habit?

9. When you think of all you have to gain, is it worth the sacrifice to follow your boundaries today?

Bible Verses

Romans 6:1-2 What shall we say then? Are we to continue in sin so that grace may increase? May it never be! How shall we who died to sin still live in it?

Romans 5:3-5 And not only this, but we also exult in our tribulations, knowing that tribulation brings about perseverance; and perseverance, proven character; and proven character, hope; and hope does not disappoint, because the love of God has been poured out within our hearts through the Holy Spirit who was given to us.

Hebrews 12:1-2a Therefore, since we have so great a cloud of witnesses surrounding us, let us also lay aside every encumbrance and the sin which so easily entangles us, and let us run with endurance the race that is set before us, fixing our eyes on Jesus, the author and perfecter of faith.

1 Peter 1:14-16 As obedient children, do not be conformed to the former lusts which were yours in your ignorance, but like the Holy One who called you, be holy yourselves also in all your behavior, because it is written, "You shall be holy, for I am holy."

Romans 13:14 But put on the Lord Jesus Christ, and make no provision for the flesh in regard to its lusts.

Tips

One woman told me it took her 30 days to finally have one day of perfectly following her boundaries. This isn't surprising. In the beginning especially it can seem almost impossible to stick to your boundaries.

One of the reasons it's so hard is because we keep telling ourselves this lie: I'll start tomorrow. Just think of it. How many times have you said, "I'll start tomorrow"? Ten times? A hundred? Hundreds? I bet most of us are in the hundreds category.

There are two reasons we say, "I'll start tomorrow." First, it allows us to do our habit without guilt. Because after all, "We'll be so good tomorrow!" And second, it allows us to postpone the suffering, because let's face it—it's hard to break habits. We know we should, but the thought of doing it is so dreadful that we look for ways to put it off. One of the ways we put it off is to reassure ourselves that we'll start tomorrow.

If we want to gain victory over our habits, we'll have to ban the phrase

"I'll start tomorrow" from our vocabulary. We can do that by answering the "I'll start tomorrow" questions every time we hear ourselves saying it. These questions will remind us of *why* we want to break our habit. We need to be reminded because our flesh is crying out "No! I want that habit! It's a great habit!"

If you can't make yourself follow your boundaries, consider getting an accountability partner: someone who will ask you every day, "Did you renew your mind?" You could also ask that person to hold you accountable to following your boundaries, but it's even more important to ask her to hold you accountable to the renewing of the mind because we're transformed by the renewing of the mind—not by following our boundaries perfectly. Thankfully!

Indulgence

1. Why don't you feel like following your boundaries today?

2. On a scale of 1 to 10, how much do you think you would enjoy your habit right now? (Think about this one.)

3. How many times would you have to break your boundaries today before you could honestly say, "That's enough. I don't want to do my habit anymore?" Be specific. *

4. If you break your boundaries, how will you feel afterwards?

    a. More satisfied than you are right now.

    b. Less satisfied than you are right now.

    c. About the same as you are right now.

    d. Wishing you could take back the whole episode.

5. How often will you follow your boundaries if you only follow them on the days you feel like following them? (Be honest.)

6. Do you think God wants you to follow your boundaries? Why or why not?

7. Are boundaries easy to follow or do you usually have to give up something to follow them?

8. What will you have to give up to follow your boundaries this time?

9. When you think of all you'll gain, is it worth the sacrifice?

* If your answer is "I'll never be satisfied," do the emotional habiting questions.

Bible Verses

Jeremiah 2:13 For My people have committed two evils: they have forsaken Me, the fountain of living waters, to hew for themselves cisterns, broken cisterns that can hold no water.

Mark 14:38 Keep watching and praying that you may not come into temptation; the spirit is willing, but the flesh is weak.

Luke 12:15 Then (Jesus) said to them, "Beware, and be on your guard against every form of greed; for not even when one has an abundance does his life consist of possessions."

Romans 13:14 But put on the Lord Jesus Christ, and make no provision for the flesh in regard to its lusts.

Philippians 3:7-8 But whatever things were gain to me, those things I have counted as loss for the sake of Christ. More than that, I count all things to be loss in view of the surpassing value of knowing Christ Jesus my Lord, for whom I have suffered the loss of all things, and count them but rubbish so that I may gain Christ.

James 1:16, 17 Do not be deceived, my beloved brethren. Every good thing given and every perfect gift is from above, coming down from the Father of lights, with whom there is no variation or shifting shadow.

1 Peter 1:14-16 As obedient children, do not be conformed to the former lusts which were yours in your ignorance, but like the Holy One who called you, be holy yourselves also in all your behavior, because it is written, "You shall be holy, for I am holy."

1 Peter 4:1-2 Therefore, since Christ has suffered in the flesh, arm yourselves also with the same purpose, because he who has suffered in the flesh has ceased from sin, so as to live the rest of the time in the flesh no longer for the lusts of men, but for the will of God.

Tips

Indulgence is an attitude that says *I want you, and I'm going to have you. I don't care if you're bad for me, I don't care if you're outside my boundaries, I just want you. And that's enough.*

It's not surprising that we feel this way since we live in a culture that tells us every day that we need to do whatever will make us happy. Because after all, isn't that what life is about—being happy?

No, that's not what life is about! Remember? Life is about loving God with all our heart, soul, mind and strength! And one of the ways we love Him well is to hold His gifts with open hands, willing to give them up at the drop of the hat. That includes our habits.

It helps to remember that we'll actually enjoy our non-sin habits more if we do them in a limited quantity. The question we need to ask is, "How much of our habit should we do? What would be best?" Since we're going to stop at some point anyway, why not stop back at the beginning, when we're still in healthy and good-for-our-relationship-with-God territory?

Justification/Denial

1. What do you feel like doing?

2. Will you break a boundary if you do that?

   a. **Yes:** If so, which boundary will you break? How were you planning to justify it? Is your justification valid? Why or why not?

   b. **No:** If not, are you breaking your boundaries in spirit even though you're not technically breaking them? Will you be more likely to break your boundaries later if you do this now? Why or why not?

3. Why do you want boundaries in this area of your life?

4. Are boundaries easy to follow, or do you usually have to give up something to follow them?

5. What will you have to give up to follow your boundaries this time?

6. What will you gain if you follow your boundaries?

7. When you think of what you'll gain, is it worth the sacrifice?

Bible Verses

Psalm 120:2 Deliver my soul, O Lord, from lying lips, from a deceitful tongue.

Psalm 139:23-24 Search me, O God, and know my heart; try me and know my anxious thoughts; and see if there be any hurtful way in me, and lead me in the everlasting way.

Romans 13:14 But put on the Lord Jesus Christ, and make no provision for the flesh in regard to its lusts.

1 Thessalonians 5:6 So then let us not sleep as others do, but let us be alert and sober.

1 Thessalonians 5:21 But examine everything carefully; hold fast to that which is good.

1 Peter 5:8 Be of sober spirit, be on the alert. Your adversary, the devil, prowls around like a roaring lion, seeking someone to devour.

Tips

The minute we set boundaries, our first impulse is to break them. Since we feel guilty about breaking them, our minds frantically (and secretly) try to come up with some justification of why in *this* situation, it's okay to break our boundaries.

One of the things it comes up with is the brilliant idea that, "Oh, I'm not really breaking my boundaries. I'm just..." And then we fill in the blank with the first thought that pops into our heads: *I'm just taking a quick look at my emails. I'm just checking to see what's on television. I'm just having a bite to see if this tastes right.*

If we want to break our habits, the first step is to be honest with ourselves: *Yes, we really are breaking our boundaries.* The next step is to realize that our boundaries are there to protect us from those times when we feel like we have a good reason to break them. If you know you're heading into a situation where you'll be tempted to justify the breaking of your boundaries, spend some time beforehand renewing your mind to prepare for that temptation.

Opportunity/Sneakiness

1. What do you feel like doing?

2. Why do you think this would be a good opportunity to break your boundaries?

3. Does God think this is a good opportunity? Why or why not?

4. Is this a good opportunity to do your habit or a dangerous situation where you'll have to be careful not to break your boundaries?

5. Can you think of anything you can do on a practical level to make it easier to follow your boundaries?

6. Go ahead and do that if you can, and then pray through the verses below for a little more strengthening.

Bible Verses

Zechariah 4:6b "Not by might nor by power, but by My Spirit," says the Lord of hosts.

1 Corinthians 10:13 No temptation has overtaken you but such as is common to man; and God is faithful, who will not allow you to be tempted beyond what you are able, but with the temptation will provide the way of escape also, so that you will be able to endure it.

Galatians 5:13 For you were called to freedom, brethren; only do not turn your freedom into an opportunity for the flesh, but through love serve one another.

Ephesians 5:8-11 For you were formerly darkness, but now you are Light in the Lord; walk as children of Light (for the fruit of the Light consists in all goodness and righteousness and truth), trying to learn what is pleasing to the Lord. Do not participate in the unfruitful deeds of darkness, but instead even expose them.

Ephesians 6:10-11 Finally, be strong in the Lord and in the strength of His might. Put on the full armor of God, so that you will be able to stand firm against the schemes of the devil.

Philippians 4:13 I can do all things through Him who strengthens me.

1 Peter 5:8 Be of sober spirit, be on the alert. Your adversary, the devil, prowls around like a roaring lion, seeking someone to devour.

Tips

If you have a habit that's shame-producing or one that someone else wants you to break, it's easy to slip into sneakiness mode, looking for opportunities to practice your habit without anyone finding out. If you struggle with sneakiness habiting, ask yourself this question: Do I really want to break this habit? If the answer is yes, then being alone is dangerous, not providential.

The best way to break free from opportunity habiting is to prepare for temptation before it hits. Here's an example: Let's say you struggle with pornography and you know your spouse or roommates will be gone for the weekend. Prepare for temptation by spending as much time as possible renewing your mind before they leave.

Write out the answers to the opportunity questions in your journal. Pray through the Bible verses. Write the verses out and place them around the house where you'll see them. Then continue renewing your mind throughout the weekend.

On a practical level, you could also plan activities away from your home so you won't be alone often or lock your iPhone and laptop in the car overnight. Or you could tell a friend and ask them to hold you accountable. If you'd like some other suggestions, read the blog post called "Preparation Truth: When Just Say No Isn't Enough" on my blog.

Reward

1. Why do you feel like you deserve a reward?

2. Will you break your boundaries if you reward yourself with your habit?

    a. **Yes:** If so, which boundary will you break? Is that a good boundary? Why or why not?

    b. **No:** If not, will you be more likely to break your boundaries later if you reward yourself with your habit now?

3. Can you think of anything else you could reward yourself with besides your habit? List a few options.

4. What will happen if you continue to reward yourself with your habit whenever you accomplish something?

5. Do you want that to happen?

6. When you think of the life you want to live, are boundaries a blessing or a curse?

7. What will you have to give up today to follow your boundaries?

8. When you think of all you'll gain by following your boundaries, is it worth the sacrifice?

Bible Verses

Colossians 3:1-2 Therefore if you have been raised up with Christ, keep seeking the things above, where Christ is, seated at the right hand of God. Set your mind on the things above, not on the things that are on earth.

Hebrews 12:1-2 Therefore, since we have so great a cloud of witnesses surrounding us, let us also lay aside every encumbrance and the sin which so easily entangles us, and let us run with endurance the race that is set before us, fixing our eyes on Jesus, the author and perfecter of faith, who for the joy set before Him endured the cross, despising the shame, and has sat down at the right hand of the throne of God.

James 1:16, 17 Do not be deceived, my beloved brethren. Every good thing given and every perfect gift is from above, coming down from the Father of lights, with whom there is no variation or shifting shadow.

Tips

In my old diet days, I'd often feel so proud of myself for sticking to my diet for one whole day that I'd think, *I deserve a reward for all that hard work!* I'd reward myself by breaking my boundaries and indulging in a nice high-calorie treat. There was just one little problem with my reward system: Not only did it send me into the I-don't-really-deserve-an-award-anymore category, it also kept me from improving my life by losing weight.

The key to gaining victory over reward habiting is to remember that boundaries make our lives *better*, not worse. And if boundaries make our lives better, then breaking them is a punishment—not a reward. If you struggle with reward habiting, try to find other ways to reward yourself. Just be careful those new ways aren't addictive!

Social

If you feel like...

1. **People are expecting you to practice your habit:** see insecurity/ people pleasing.

2. **People will condemn you or get mad at you if you don't practice your habit with them:** see fear of condemnation or worry.

3. **You have a right to practice your habit because everyone else is doing it:** see entitlement.

4. **You want to practice your habit because it wouldn't be any fun if you couldn't:** see indulgence or greed/lust.

5. **It's not a big deal if you break your boundaries since it's a social occasion:** see carelessness.

Tips

It's hard to say no to our habits when everyone around us is engaging in them. If you're going to a social event where you'll be tempted to break your boundaries, renew your mind beforehand so you'll have a better chance of following your boundaries. It may also be helpful to pray through the Bible verses below as they'll help you focus on loving the people at the gathering, rather than doing your habit at the gathering! Depending on what your habit is, you may also want to think about skipping the social occasion.

Bible Verses

1 Corinthians 13:4-7 Love is patient, love is kind and is not jealous; love does not brag and is not arrogant, does not act unbecomingly; it does not seek its own, is not provoked, does not take into account a wrong suffered, does not rejoice in unrighteousness, but rejoices with the truth; bears all things, believes all things, hopes all things, endures all things.

Colossians 3:12-15 So, as those who have been chosen of God, holy and beloved, put on a heart of compassion, kindness, humility, gentleness and patience; bearing with one another, and forgiving each other, whoever has a complaint against anyone; just as the Lord forgave you, so also should you. Beyond all these things put on love, which is the perfect bond of unity. Let the peace of Christ rule in your hearts, to which indeed you were called in one body; and be thankful.

Tired of the Struggle

1. Do you ever wish life were easier?

2. Why do you think it's so hard to break this habit?

3. If you look at the people around you who are trying to break this habit, do you find that most of them have an easy time of it? If not, what do you find?

4. Do you think God wants you to continue working on breaking this habit even though it's so hard? Why or why not?

5. How do you think God feels when He sees you suffering? (Hebrews 4:15)

6. Who are you in His eyes? (Turn to the insecurity/feeling inadequate verses for the answer to this question.)

7. What do you think He wants to do for you in the midst of your struggle? (See insecurity verses for ideas.)

8. What do you think He wants *you* to do in the midst of your struggle? (Ephesians 6:11-18, Romans 12:2, 2 Corinthians 10:3-5)

9. What will you gain if you go to Him for help with this struggle?

10. When you think of all you'll gain, is it worth taking the time to fight the battle with spiritual weapons?

11. Would it help to have someone hold you accountable to the renewing of the mind? If so, whom could you ask?

Bible Verses

Psalm 30:5b Weeping may last for the night, but a shout of joy comes in the morning.

Romans 6:1-2 What shall we say then? Are we to continue in sin so that grace may increase? May it never be! How shall we who died to sin still live in it?

2 Corinthians 10:3-5 For though we walk in the flesh, we do not war according to the flesh, for the weapons of our warfare are not of the flesh, but divinely powerful for the destruction of fortresses. We are destroying speculations and every lofty thing raised up against the knowledge of God, and we are taking every thought captive to the obedience of Christ.

Galatians 6:9 Let us not lose heart in doing good, for in due time we will reap if we do not grow weary.

Philippians 1:6 For I am confident of this very thing, that He who began a good work in you will perfect it until the day of Christ Jesus.

Philippians 3:13-14 Brethren, I do not regard myself as having laid hold of it yet; but one thing I do: forgetting what lies behind and reaching forward to what lies ahead, I press on toward the goal for the prize of the upward call of God in Christ Jesus.

Hebrews 4:15-16 For we do not have a high priest who cannot sympathize with our weaknesses, but One who has been tempted in all things as we are, yet without sin. Therefore let us draw near with confidence to the throne of grace, so that we may receive mercy and find grace to help in time of need.

Hebrews 12:1-2a Therefore, since we have so great a cloud of witnesses surrounding us, let us also lay aside every encumbrance and the sin which so easily entangles us, and let us run with endurance the race that is set before us, fixing our eyes on Jesus, the author and perfecter of faith.

Hebrews 12:3 For consider Him who has endured such hostility by sinners against Himself, so that you will not grow weary and lose heart. You have not yet resisted to the point of shedding blood in your striving against sin.

Hebrews 12:11 All discipline for the moment seems not to be joyful, but sorrowful; yet to those who have been trained by it, afterwards it yields the peaceful fruit of righteousness.

Tips

Let's face it. It's hard to keep dealing with the same problem over and over again. Sometimes we feel like throwing in the towel and just *giving up*.

Don't do it.

Spiritual battles are just what they're called: battles. And battles aren't easy. You can't enter into battle without entering into suffering. Here's a comforting thought, though. It's far better to suffer *with* God than without Him. Spiritual battles can be intense, sweet times of fellowship with God—so sweet it almost feels like it's worth struggling through the problem just to have those times with God.

I want to encourage you to keep going to Him for help. Renew your mind. Take off those lies and put on the truth. Let the Holy Spirit work in you and minister to you and conform you to His image. The journey won't be pleasant, but *afterwards*, you'll experience the peaceful fruit of righteousness (Hebrews 12:11). And that will be worth the struggle.

Other Resources

Leader's Guide

If you'd like to lead a group study with this book, you can download a free leader's guide at barbraveling.com under the Renewing of the Mind Project tab.

Other Books by Barb Raveling

Freedom from Emotional Eating. Although this book is directed towards weight loss, the majority of the book is about breaking free from negative emotions, so it may be helpful if you're doing an emotions project.

Taste for Truth: A 30 Day Weight Loss Bible Study. Although this book is geared toward breaking an overeating habit, you could also use it to break other habits. Most of the lessons will still apply, no matter what type of habit you're trying to break.

I Deserve a Donut (And Other Lies That Make You Eat). This book is similar to *The Renewing of the Mind Project.* It contains the emotions questions and Bible verses that are in this book and another set of questions similar to the breaking a habit questions in this book that are geared specifically to an overeating habit.

I hope to write more Bible studies on habits and emotions. If you'd like to hear more about future studies, sign up for my author page at amazon.com or my blog posts at barbraveling.com

Apps

I Deserve a Donut is also available as an Android and iPhone app.

Free Resources

- Barb's podcast, *The Christian Habits Podcast*. This podcast features interviews with people who are working on renewing of the mind projects and other interviews and episodes on habits, emotions, the renewing of the mind and other related topics.

- Barb's blog at barbraveling.com. This has articles and Bible studies on various topics related to your projects.

- The Renewing of the Mind Tools tab at barbraveling.com. This has articles on other tools you can use to renew your mind.

- The Renewing of the Mind Bible Study Series. Look for this under the Free Bible Study tab at barbraveling.com. It includes several Bible studies and a four-week plan for the renewing of the mind that you could use alongside your project if you'd like.

Resources by Other Authors

- There are all kinds of great resources out there by other authors. Because the types of projects you'll be doing are so varied, it would be difficult to list all of the resources in this book. Ask your local Christian bookstore for recommendations, as they'll be up on the latest books. Your church librarian or pastor may also be able to recommend helpful books for you in the area of your project. I will also try to include resources on my blog as I find them.

Accountability Chart

One of the hardest things about the renewing of the mind is making yourself do it. Sometimes it helps to record your sessions on a chart. I've included six charts in this book for that purpose. You can also download charts at the Renewing of the Mind tab at my blog.

Use the chart to record what you did to renew your mind each day, in addition to regular quiet times and talking to God throughout the day. I've included a sample chart below.

In this chart, the person made a goal to renew her mind twice a day. On Monday, she truth journaled and went through the people pleasing questions. On Tuesday, she went through the anger and judgment questions. On Wednesday she went through the people pleasing questions twice.

Whenever you do something new to renew your mind, just jot it down on the next line and put an x in the appropriate column. For Scripture meditation and prayer, you can either have a general Scripture meditation and prayer line, or you could include them in the different categories, such as pride or judgment.

At the end of the week, record what God taught you that week. It may also help to record how diligent you were with the renewing of the mind, not to be legalistic, but just so you can be aware of your progress.

Week 1	M	T	W	Th	F	S	S
Insecurity/People Pleasing	x		xx				
Truth Journaling	x					x	
Anger/Annoyance		x			x	x	
Judgment		x		x			xx
Scripture Prayer					x		x

Week 1	M	T	W	Th	F	S	S

On a scale of 1 to 10, how diligent were you with the renewing of the mind this week?

What did God teach you this week?

Week 2	M	T	W	Th	F	S	S

On a scale of 1 to 10, how diligent were you with the renewing of the mind this week?

What did God teach you this week?

Week 3	M	T	W	Th	F	S	S

On a scale of 1 to 10, how diligent were you with the renewing of the mind this week?

What did God teach you this week?

Week 4	M	T	W	Th	F	S	S

On a scale of 1 to 10, how diligent were you with the renewing of the mind this week?

What did God teach you this week?

Week 5	M	T	W	Th	F	S	S

On a scale of 1 to 10, how diligent were you with the renewing of the mind this week?

What did God teach you this week?

Week 6	M	T	W	Th	F	S	S

On a scale of 1 to 10, how diligent were you with the renewing of the mind this week?

What did God teach you this week?

Acknowledgments

I am so grateful to the following people who have helped me with the writing of this book. Thank you...

- Scott, for your patience, for all the hours you put in editing, and for testing the book out with your own project. You're the best!

- Tanya, for your wisdom, friendship, and for encouraging me to write this book years ago. I finally wrote it!

- Kayt, for all your fun little comments and a great job editing. You gave me encouragement when I needed it.

- Martha, for asking me to lead a study on this at the exact time I needed it, for being such an encouragement, and for giving me fun breaks at the coffee shop!

- Lynette, Lisa, Carol Ann, Jennifer, Tati, April, Ginny, Martha, Patti, Lois, Marci, Nancy, Pam, and Virgie for coming to the Bible study, testing out the project, and giving me encouragement and feedback. This book wouldn't be the same without you.

- Christina and Barb for your encouragement, friendship, and help with accountability. I would have wasted far more time if you two hadn't been holding me accountable!

- Deborah, for your encouragement and help with editing in the midst of harvest.

- Steve, for so many great book designs that I had a hard time choosing just one!

- My fellow bloggers: Heidi, Melanie, Elizabeth, TC, Floyd, Caleb, Ngina, Dan, Loren, Bernard, Deb, Kari, Betty, and Karen. Thanks so much for encouraging me, sharing my books, and writing reviews for me. Getting to know all of you has been one of the best parts about writing, and I so appreciate all of you!

- And last but not least, all of you wonderful readers! Thanks for encouraging me with your emails, reviews, and comments. I'm privileged to write for you, and I hope this book is a blessing to you!

If I've forgotten anyone, please forgive me. I appreciate you even though I am such a forgetful person!

About the Author

Barb grew up in North Dakota and attended the University of Montana where she majored in home economics education and business management. After graduating from college with two degrees, she got a job as a waitress (which she loved) and then got married. After a short banking career, she and her husband had the first of four kids and Barb entered the stay-at-home mom life, later graduating to the homeschool mom life.

While homeschooling, she organized co-ops, taught speech and interpersonal communication classes, and led Bible studies for her kids and their friends. After homeschooling for 22 years, Barb and her husband are now empty nesters and enjoying their clean (but far too quiet) home. In their spare time, they like to hike, camp, ski, backpack, sit by the fire and read, and hang out with family and friends.